Praise for
Does This Baby Make Me Look Straight?

"I read Dan's compelling and 'modern' book in almost one sitting, and when my face wasn't in my hands laughing myself silly, I was touched and moved by Dan's ability to stay in his heart."

—Jane Lynch

"Okay. I know Dan. We've worked together for almost ten years. I've never seen him naked. But after reading his book, I feel like I've seen him without a stitch, no cover, completely bare. I also saw myself in this as a parent and thought, 'Oh, I'm not alone with my thoughts.' It's good not to be all alone with these feelings and as is usual for me, Dan is the perfect company to keep."

—Lisa Kudrow

"Few people make me laugh as much as Dan Bucatinsky, but I was not prepared this time to be crying between the guffaws. This is a book I will return to again and again for its humor—that's a no-brainer—but for its sly wisdom as well."

—Terrence McNally, Tony Award–winning playwright

"I had every intention of simply enjoying this book on the toilet, but after reading the first page it went to my nightstand and from there to the family room, where I read paragraphs out loud to friends. This book is hysterically funny and beyond bold. Dan Bucatinsky just goes for it and says the things you didn't realize you were thinking."

—Max Mutchnick, creator of *Will and Grace*

"Loved how Dan bounced from crazy silly to gut-wrenching and heartwarming. His humor was the sugar that made the crystal meth of his life go down. I will be a better parent because he went places and made some mistakes so I don't have to. Adoption is so difficult and just being in a relationship is hard enough, but as he made clear in the book, so frickin' worth it."

—Tom Arnold

"This is a smart, funny, relatable, and altogether human book. How are families made? With love, and courage, and laughter, and grace—all abundantly present in this terrific story. I wish Dan Bucatinsky lived next door to me so we could kvell and kvetch together about our beautiful kids and the complexities of modern parenthood."

—Dani Shapiro, author of the
bestselling memoir *Slow Motion*

"Once I put my kid to bed, this book made me laugh out loud late into the night. The perils of parenting as told by Dan are hilarious and heartbreaking and utterly recognizable to anyone who has a child. Brilliant."

—Shonda Rhimes, creator of *Grey's Anatomy*

"I devoured this book. I love Dan's story, his kids, and his writing."

—Jennifer Garner

does this baby make me look straight?

Confessions of a Gay Dad

DAN BUCATINSKY

A TOUCHSTONE BOOK
Published by Simon & Schuster
New York London Toronto Sydney New Delhi

Touchstone
A Division of Simon & Schuster, Inc.
1230 Avenue of the Americas
New York, NY 10020

Certain names and identifying characteristics have been changed, certain characters and events have been combined and compressed, and comedic license has been taken.

First Touchstone trade paperback edition June 2012

TOUCHSTONE and colophon are registered trademarks of Simon & Schuster, Inc.

For information about special discounts for bulk purchases, please contact Simon & Schuster Special Sales at 1-866-506-1949 or business@simonandschuster.com.

The Simon & Schuster Speakers Bureau can bring authors to your live event. For more information or to book an event contact the Simon & Schuster Speakers Bureau at 1-866-248-3049 or visit our website at www.simonspeakers.com.

Designed by Joy O'Meara

Manufactured in the United States of America

1 3 5 7 9 10 8 6 4 2

Library of Congress Cataloging-in-Publication Data
Bucatinsky, Dan.
Does this baby make me look straight?: confessions of a gay dad / Dan Bucatinsky. —1st ed.
p. cm.
1. Gay fathers. 2. Parenting. I. Title.
HQ76.13.B83 2012
306.874′208664—dc23 2011050819

ISBN 978-1-4516-6073-9
ISBN 978-1-4516-6074-6 (ebook)

For Don Roos, my kids' Papi,
and in memory of Julio Bucatinsky, my Papi

CONTENTS

chapter one

Wake Up and Smell the Fingers

Daddy?"

I'm in my five-year-old daughter Eliza's bathroom rinsing her toothbrush when I hear her chirp from behind me on the toilet.

Even now I'm oddly caught off guard sometimes by the title "Daddy," as though I'm suddenly looking down at a new suit I don't ever remember putting on. But I like it. It fits me. Makes me look thinsy.

"Yes, monkey?" I reply, distractedly.

She holds her fingers up to my face. Then come three tiny words. Oh, how those words repeat in my head, over and over again, echoing in slow motion: *"Smell . . . my . . . fingers . . ."* Nothing good ever comes after those words.

I flash to where her fingers may have been. A field of lavender would be my first choice. But that's not likely at this late hour. Any chance it's the perfume counter at Bloomingdale's? No. She doesn't have her driver's license yet. She's five, remember? My brain is losing its desperate battle to steer away from the more likely candidates.

On the one hand, I don't want her to feel any embarrassment or guilt. Her body is her temple. It's all beautiful. And my love for it and her is unconditional. On the other hand? Smell your own damn fingers, kid. What about me looks like I'd *like* to smell your fingers? Tell me now so I can change it immediately and no one ever makes this mistake again.

But there's no time to get into all that. I find myself obliging. I hold her adorable, glitter-nail-polished fingers to my face and I smell. There's definitely something there. Some smell. What is that? Is it ass? Could be.

"What is that, darling?" I ask, trying to hide my anxiety, although my voice is starting to climb north.

Eliza giggles. "It's my tushy, Daddy." Okay. Not great news. In fact, I feel light-headed. But it's not her fault. Maybe she hasn't mastered the finer points of the bum wipe. We're in the early days of this particular skill set, even though she is five.

"Darling, we don't touch our bum-bums, okay? Did the toilet paper slip? That happens, sweetie, but with practice—"

"No, Daddy," she says with a conspiratorial grin. "It's my *front* tushy."

I don't know what happens next because I've blacked out. The room is spinning. Images flash from my past—or maybe somebody else's past, I'm too panicked to watch carefully.

All I can think is *How?* How the hell did I end up here, in this particular conversation, with this little girl, holding these particular fingers up to this face? I can't seem to remember the series of events that led to this moment. Any of them. It is the same sensation I have after plowing through four bowls of cereal while watching *The Biggest Loser.*

Even though it feels like I was somehow propelled through time and space and then plopped unceremoniously in this moment, in this bathroom, with this funky-fingered cherub smiling up at me, I know it happened in real time. Evolving into the man I've become: the son, the husband, the "Daddy." It was life, happening one terrifying moment at a time, the result of big decisions and small ones, some easy and some daunting as hell.

I guess the Big Bang would have to have been around the filming of *Under the Tuscan Sun*. I had two and a half minutes of screen time with Diane Lane, which thankfully took six weeks to shoot in a beautiful countryside in Tuscany. I had become quite close with the director, Audrey Wells, who was there with her two-year-old daughter. She spied me playing with little Tatiana and asked if I'd ever thought about having kids. The answer of course was yes. I had. But my boyfriend had mixed feelings. (Ah, it's been almost twenty years, I shouldn't say "boyfriend." I should say "partner." Too cold. "Lover"? No. Too moist. Okay, "husband," but only in California ever since Tom Arnold agreed to marry us on the patio of our house, our two kids as witnesses, only a few weeks before Prop 8 went into effect in 2008.) Don and I always managed to come up with perfectly good reasons why we shouldn't have kids. Audrey, though, proceeded to give me an impassioned speech about "discovering the father in one another," which really got to me. I remember calling Don from a pay phone and yelling, "I want to discover the father in—" *Click.* The line went dead as I ran out of minutes on my calling card.

It took about a year for Don and me to get on the same page. After all, our options were limited. We couldn't just "forget" to take a pill. Don kept waiting for someone to leave a newborn in a basket on our doorstep. Our close friends Michael and Mary urged him to be a tiny bit more proactive.

"That's bullshit!" I remember them saying. "Nobody is going to leave a kid at your feet. If that's how you really feel, go out there and get your baby!" It was all Don needed to hear, apparently, his "aha" moment. Because after that we started making the necessary calls.

Surrogacy was the popular option. But Don was convinced we'd wind up using *my* sperm and he'd instantly feel left out by the two-against-one shenanigans. He grew up with two brothers and avoids triangulation at all costs. More importantly, he was uncomfortable with the idea of surrogacy, felt it was nothing more than "womb leasing" and wanted no part of it. I knew adoption was the only other choice. And since there are so many children being born every day who need parents, we both thought this would be the best. I'd be lying, though, if I didn't say I had some hidden trepidation.

I don't like to admit it but I was petrified about my own ability to bond with an adopted baby, a child with no genetic ties to me. It was lack of experience, really. Maybe ignorance. Fear? *What will it smell like?* I'd think. *How will the baby know I'm its daddy?* Let's face it: I was an idiot. That was until the day of the birth. The second Eliza was lifted into the air, like Kunta Kinte in *Roots*, I fell in love. And I mean that *second.* Which made the road to get there, worth every gut-wrenching, nerve-wracking, tear-squirting moment.

The process of making an adoption plan isn't easy. For anyone. But for same-sex couples, it's even more of a challenge. Foreign adoptions for the "gays" are impossible these days. Homophobia is more the rule than the exception. In most parts of the world, like China and Guatemala, the words "I'm a man looking to adopt a baby" must be the same as "Sociopath seeks naked hugs and finger fun!"

No. Our best bet was something called open adoption, where we'd be chosen by a birth mother and then keep in some contact so that our child would have a healthy understanding of who she is and where she came from. At least, that's our hope. We needed information. And courage. So we talked with other couples who had adopted and read every book we could find. We derived not a small amount of inspiration from Dan Savage's book *The Kid*—a wonderfully funny and honest account of his and his partner's journey through the adoption process.

After a meeting with an adoption lawyer, background checks, fingerprinting, and registering with a family services agency, the very next step was creating a "birth mother letter." It was more of a brochure where we described ourselves, our relationship and our life together as a way of enticing birth moms to call us. Smile till it hurts. Don and I struggled with this process for several weeks. I mean, how could we paint an accurate picture of ourselves in a way that communicates what perfect parents we thought we could be without sounding immodest or entitled or, you know, not gay-gay?

The key was to understand what kind of person our birth mom might be. Our lawyer told us that the majority come from Vegas and usually fall into one of two categories: the college coed or the stripper. Believe it or not, he said we'd be better off with a stripper. The coeds, he said, often had multiple partners, were binge drinkers and in denial about being pregnant at least until after finals. Strippers, he said, were more responsible and used fewer substances. I guess it's not so easy to swing naked from a pole on crystal meth. Naturally, Don and I were all about tailoring our brochure for our particular exotic-dancing birth mom. But where would we start? How much should we let her know? I was dying to tell her about my first professional showbiz job as a backup singer/dancer for a *Playboy* playmate in a hideously tacky variety show called *Truly Outrageous.* Don was adamant I bury those details with the sequined wrestling singlet I wore for our "Steam Heat" number.

"How do you know she won't respond to that?" I asked.

"How well did people respond who saw the show?" he asked. Good point. My parents, who came out to see their son in his first professional job as an entertainer since graduating from Vassar, described it as "not their cup of tea." Generous, I think, given the racy show was a "one-night-only" engagement, at midnight, on Yom Kippur—the most solemn and holy of Jewish holidays. The show *was* truly outrageous and not in the way that might help us get a baby. No. We had no strategy which highlighted the fact we had no real idea who our birth mom was.

Don thought he knew: she was a thirty-eight-year-old mother of two who did volunteer work during the day and only stripped at night to put food on the table. Yeah, okay. Uh-huh. I was convinced I knew strippers better than Don. After all, I was the one who went to a Vegas bachelor party for my friend John a few years back and saw, much to my horror, a girl named Phenomenon pour ginger ale through her vajayjay and into John's mouth. I was pretty sure she wasn't wrapping up her gig at Nude Awakening to race home and put the kids to bed so she could finish her thesis on Chaucer.

"We should write that we like the outdoors," I said, as we opened a blank page on the computer to write our BML (birth mother letter).

"No. We're not writing that," Don argued. "We may as well say we're Navy SEALs or circus clowns." Don hates the outdoors. He likes big, dark hotel rooms, room service, and twenty-four-hour HGTV.

"Put down water-skiing!" I said.

He rolled his eyes. "You haven't water-skied in twenty years." He wasn't wrong. But what version of "me" did I want the stripper to know? I mean, I do love water-skiing. That was the truth. So what if I hadn't done it in a long . . . *long* time? Better than what Don wanted to put in the letter:

"Hello. My name is Donald. I've always been a movie buff and an avid reader. I love Jane Austen. And I don't know how to throw overhand."

"No way!" I argued. "May as well write 'Your baby will be a class A nerd, destined to be stuffed in lockers and toilets.' No. Even I wouldn't give my baby to that."

"At least it's honest," he defended his position.

"So? Are you trying to have a family or give a deposition?" I said, self-righteously.

If we went with the truth, the whole truth, and nothing but the truth, we'd have to say we preferred malls over museums, we worshipped at the altar of TiVo, and while we loved movies and documentaries, who were we kidding? More often than not we could be found watching *Amazing Race, Project Runway*, and *Intervention*, a show with gut-wrenching stories of young people shooting up in a Taco Bell bathroom before being forced to get clean! Now *that's* entertainment.

Next came the grueling task of picking photos to include in this brochure. Dan in front of Harrods in London. Don on a quaint street in Rome. "See, birth mom? With Don and Dan, your baby will get to see the world!"

We wanted her to know we could be good male role models even though our only relationship to sports was watching figure skating on TV and making fart noises with every triple salchow. That's not gonna get us a kid. Instead we had to turn to the hard sell. Here's an actual quote from our BML:

"Dear Birth Mom: First of all, we want to thank you. We know there are many couples asking you to consider them and so we want to say how much we appreciate you taking the time to read our letter."

I read it back, horrified by how we sounded: *We know you have a choice when it comes to air travel. Thanks for choosing Dan and Don Air!*

Whatever we did, it worked. Twice. First, with a young woman from Las Vegas who was three months pregnant and picked us to adopt her baby. It didn't ultimately work out. But on my birthday in September of 2004, we got a call from a plucky yet sweet nineteen-year-old, already a mother of twins, from Wisconsin who *did* want to fly Dan and Don Air. Her name, let's say, was Monica. And she wasn't a stripper. And she didn't care about our brochure. She picked us because she and her mom were fans of the television show

Queer Eye for the Straight Guy and thought we'd make "ahh-some dads."

I'll never forget the day we first laid eyes on Monica, coming down the escalator at LAX. We'd talked on the phone a bunch of times and we'd noticed how she had a loud, slow, gruff voice. Her mother told us she got nervous around new people and did not like to be photographed. We immediately pictured a clinically obese girl with thick glasses and a stained Hello Kitty sweatshirt, teetering on the edge of "mentally challenged." She turned out to be a beautiful, wide-eyed, tough-talking, pack-a-day teen in stretch jeans and her boyfriend's football jacket, as if she had literally been conjured from the pages of a Don Roos screenplay. Chain-smoking and Slurpee-drinking, Monica was the epitome of "street smart." She was affable, confident and had an enormous heart. She was, she *is*, affectionate, stubborn, playful, proud, funny, opinionated, and of course, generous. The sacrifice she was able to endure? I am forever changed by her and inspired by her strength and courage. Okay, she could've learned a thing or two about birth control. But she always insisted "birth control just doesn't work" on her! I kept wondering if it wouldn't have worked better had she remembered to take it out of the box and put it in. Or on. But then, imagine if she had? Unfathomable. It was Monica's lack of impulse control that made the creation of our family possible.

The whole experience bonded us. And then, in that delivery room Don, Monica, and I held hands as first Eliza and then, two years later, Jonah were cut from their umbilical cord–and from their nine-month lifeline to Cinnabons, Mountain Dew, and Marlboro Menthols. Tears streamed down all our cheeks. It was clear, as sentimental as it may sound, that our kids were born out of the hearts of three people. Not just two of us. And not just the one.

It's funny, though, becoming a "Daddy." I fully expected to discover what that director had spoken to me about, the "father within." But what I never imagined—what I could *never* have ever predicted—was finding the *mother* within me. There is no doubt that when Eliza got home, I fully took on the role of mother to my cub. If I could have stuck a boob in her, I would have. And I always became defensive when people assumed I didn't know what I was doing. Like when we would be traveling and *every woman on the plane* would offer us important advice, like "Don't forget to feed her" or "Air pressure makes baby's ears go ouchy." I'd be, like, "Really? And here I was about to stuff her in the overhead compartment!"

It's like that Elizabeth Stone quote: being a parent is like deciding to "have your heart go walking around outside your body." I wanted the world to know that something had changed in me. Shifted. On a cellular level. Something that made certain things like her gestures, smells, and particular smiles make me want to burst into tears. What is that? Sadness? Joy? Pride? Being a parent.

• • •

Back in the bathroom, Eliza looks up at me with a little shrug. It's cute. But clearly I'm meant to do something, say something. I wasn't prepared for this. Why wasn't this in any of the books we read prior to having kids?

"Hey, listen, polka dot. It's your body and you're the boss of it. Yeah? But not so much with the fingers in your, you know, front tushy, okay? You just want to keep all of your areas, um, clean."

Not bad, given I had no lead time to prepare my response. Anyway, it'll have to do. But let's face it. "Front tushy" instead of just saying "vagina"? I got work to do.

chapter two

This CAN'T Be Love

It was the fall of 1992, and I'd recently moved from New York to Los Angeles for a one-year trial to kick-start my acting and writing career in film and television. I was performing, but not making money performing, a two-person show I'd written about relationships and love—a topic I realize now I knew absolutely *nothing* about.

To pay the rent I got hooked up by a friend with the glamorous job of selling pencils, CDs, and T-shirts for the musical *Forever Plaid* at the Canon Theatre in Beverly Hills, which is now the Montage Hotel. To this day, whenever I'm in that hotel's lobby, I feel the impulse to ask people if they want "small, medium, or large."

That Valentine's Day, I began a sneaky little affair with this guy—I'll call him David—who also worked at the theater. David had a house, dogs, a coffeemaker—oh, and he wore a gold band so he also had a husband. Oops. For some reason, these were all things I found *very* attractive, perhaps in their power to symbolize the guy's capacity to love. I had never before given much thought to having a relationship. It certainly wasn't that high up on my list. I was always far more focused on my career. But the feelings I had for David were bigger than me. I thought only about him. It felt like there was a magnetic force drawing us together. And when we were apart, I was counting the minutes until I'd see him again. I guess it was as close to a drug addiction as I've ever come.

Oh my God, I thought to myself, *this must be love.* I felt powerless in the face of it. And, at the same time, so relieved that I was capable of it. For years I had feared I just wasn't cut out for love.

Our relationship was all very passionate and exciting except for those times we'd be in his car and he'd see someone he knew and make me duck down by the floor mats. With some dried mud and a piece of gravel against my skin, it occurred to me: *This can't be love, can it?* But I somehow convinced myself to keep going. I was young. And I believed David's assertion that he was capable of loving two guys at the same time. All that, paired with my powerlessness over the seductive nature of our affair, convinced me that what I was experiencing was the very definition of "true love."

Six months later, I'd grown some balls. Not a lot. Maybe more like *a* ball. It was enough to break up for the third and last time: "If you aren't ready to choose me over Tom, then we must never, ever speak to each other again." We burst into tears. We might as well have burst into flames: it was a ridiculous, can't-catch-your-breath, over-the-top, way-too-gay kind of grief. I fell to the ground as I looked up to the skies and thought, *WHY? Why is this happening to me? And why is there always gravel digging into my skin?*

A short ten days later, I'm trying to keep busy at the theater box office, listening to Bonnie Raitt's "I Can't Make You Love Me" on a loop. I'm not just riding the self-pity bus but driving it—feeling sorry for my sad, puffy-eyed, pathetic self. That's when my close friend Linda walked into the box office to invite me to play Celebrity with a bunch of her friends. She didn't hide the fact that she was using the party as a chance to fix me up with a thirty-seven-year-old screenwriter named Don. She was, however, ignoring the fact he didn't want to date someone so young and an actor. I didn't want to date anyone so much older and well established. She was also ignoring the fact I was in mourning over the end of my love affair and trying to nurse my broken heart. I was shocked she'd think I could date anyone so soon after the breakup—or *ever again.* I went anyway, grateful for the distraction and free food.

I was most definitely the youngest person in the room and, besides Don, the only other guy. It was a circle of women, Don's closest friends, sitting on the couch like a quilting bee, a firing squad, or perhaps a judges' table. One woman in particular was sitting on the floor, leaning against the couch, where Don sat giving her a back rub. She was—how should I put this gently—*very* plain-looking. She was heavy, with thick eyeglasses, too-short hair, and a big gummy-tooth smile. Within a minute I got the story: her name was Mimi, she was dying of cancer, and Don was her primary caregiver. Hi! Welcome to the party!

I'd never met a dying person before. I remember feeling suffocated by the information, like it was way over my head and out of my comfort zone. *Just get through the night and you never have to see any of these people again,* I thought. As I mentioned, I was still in my twenties and easily intimidated. Scared, maybe, I wouldn't be able to rise to the challenge. Or maybe scared the whole dying thing might somehow rub off on me.

As it turned out, I liked Don. We got each other's sense of humor and could talk really easily. Over the next few weeks, Don and I spoke on the phone almost every night. We finally met for coffee and I had the super awesome good sense to spend every minute talking about David and my broken heart. Don tried hard to hide his rolling "check please" eyes. I couldn't imagine why he'd give me another chance, but he did.

We made a date to have dinner. We met at an Italian restaurant in West Hollywood. He apologized for being late, as he'd had to stop at Mimi's to bring her food and cigarettes. Yes. Don and Mimi were smokers at the time. Benson & Hedges 100's Menthol. Cartons of them. It confused me.

"Should she be smoking with, you know, cancer?" I asked.

Don shrugged. "Well, what's the point? She's terminal. And she knows it. Who am I to police her?"

I kicked myself. Like maybe if I had an ounce of compassion, I would've thought of that. Don was the manager of her care, and I decided to leave it alone. I had just returned from New York, so I brought him a bag of Zabar's coffee. He brought me a pack of cigarettes. We sat on the patio and smoked. Clearly, or perhaps ironically, back then, smoking was reserved for those he cared the most about.

Don was a real grown-up—smart, confident, and blessed with a magnanimous personality. He's always been funny, sharp-witted, and unapologetically honest. One had to have a tough skin around him. His verbal sparring was hilarious but could leave a mark. He'd even joke about Mimi's illness, which surprisingly put everyone, especially Mimi, at ease. After another bad doctor's report, Don would simply ask, "Honey, why *does* God hate you so much? Maybe he's jealous of all the attention." Or he'd tell her, "Hey. Quit whining, will you? It's not like you're dying. Oh, wait. You are." And she'd laugh and laugh. Or she'd be stuffing her face with donuts: "Don't hold back, angel, those tumors need their strength!" It was disarming. But it also took the ominous tension right out of the situation. Mimi just loved it. We all did, the seven of us who came together to help Don take care of Mimi.

I loved his rough edges paired with such sweetness and generosity. I'd never met anyone like him before. I knew I wanted to pursue a relationship with Don. In my head. My heart, however, was still pining for David, who was no longer even living in L.A.

Don knew I thought he'd be good for me. "The healthy choice," he called it. Nutritious. Like he was the oat bran muffin with omega-3s rather than the caramel chocolate donut with buttercream frosting. Making matters worse and conspiring against our relationship, Mimi's health was deteriorating. The more involved Don became with me, the needier Mimi was becoming. Not so odd, actually, as we all knew she was in love with him. And why wouldn't she be?

Her own family had disowned her for reasons I didn't quite understand. She seemed to have only Don in her life. And his friends. And now, me. Don had spent a year taking her to support groups or waiting outside hospitals. He even took her to Lourdes, even though she was Jewish, because she read an article about the healing effects of bathing in the holy water. She was getting desperate for a cure. And he was committed to learning how to "care with respect" as he had learned in Shanti. "Let the patient be in charge of her own illness," they told him. "Never try to know more than she knows . . ." Patients talk to their own doctors and make decisions about their own care. Don had learned from his mistakes. He'd had two friends die of AIDS and gotten too involved in the medical side of their care. He was determined to do it right this time.

I learned, slowly, how to be a caregiver. But I felt awkward and ill-equipped, at best. Impatient and mean, at my worst. *Just* die *already*, I'd think to myself when she'd hijack a romantic weekend in New York by keeping Don on the phone to describe the consistency and frequency of her poop. I'd get so mad. And then furious and depressed about being the guy who was wishing a dying woman would just get to it. I'd wonder what she'd do if we weren't around to help her. My thoughts ran like a news ticker in my brain: *Who else could she call? And why doesn't she call them right now? Why doesn't she ever feel guilty? And why is she so fucking fat after all that chemo?*

I began to question everything. Maybe I didn't know what love was after all. Maybe I was incapable of *real* love—of nurturing. Though having kids was the furthest thing from my mind at that time, I do remember wondering if I would ever have a parental bone in my body, given my inability to care for Mimi and nurture her and love her unconditionally. But it all felt too intimate, intense, and ultimately sad. I wanted out. And Don sensed I had one foot out the door. But his closest friend, Susan, and my friends Linda and Jodi worked tirelessly to encourage each of us to stay the course.

They all seemed to feel that Don and I belonged together and so we went on blind faith and stuck it out. Much to Mimi's dismay. She resented me despite my efforts to help her, bring her lunch or groceries when she was on bed rest. She tried to act like she liked me. But after a minute or two, all conversation would turn to *our* boyfriend "Donny." How I hated how she said that *Don-ny.* "Where's Donny?" "What's Donny doing now?" "Could you evaporate and rematerialize as Donny?" That last one she said with her eyes.

Six months into my relationship with Donny, on Valentine's Day, I heard from David. We spoke and I felt . . . normal. Two people making small talk. There was no power in our conversation. No heat to speak of. Just two old friends. I was so relieved it was finally over. I wondered if it had ever really been love or was it some unconscious wish for me to be the kind of guy who could find love and succumb to it? But then look what happened: I had stopped trying so hard and, at long last, I had fallen in love. With Don. Despite the gravitational pull of Mimi's progressing disease.

By April or May, Mimi was walking with crutches, had lost her sight in one eye—and had daily episodes of extreme cramping that, luckily for me, could be abated only by Don spooning with her and rubbing her back.

"She has *brain* tumors. Why does she have cramps all over her body?" I asked. The chemo, asshole! Of course. Don was so patient with her. But I couldn't stand how much time and physical attention she needed. And she was so unapologetic. I was sure that if I were in her position, I'd be embarrassed to keep asking for more. I spent hours imagining what I wished Mimi might say: *No. I'll be fine. Go to the movies with your boyfriend. For God's sake, you've only been together for six months. If I need anything, I'll call. Go. That Danny is so cute! And funny. And smart.* Yeah. No. Those words were never said.

One morning, she called us in a panic, screaming. Her hair was coming out in clumps. We brought in a hairstylist friend to shave her head. Don held her hands and wiped her tears as the hair fell to the ground. I watched from the other room, my own tears hidden from view. That night, Linda took Mimi to see her friend at the time, Liza Minnelli, in concert. They went backstage afterward, and Liza, moved by Mimi's story, taught her how to twist scarves attractively around her bald head. Mimi beamed with excitement. The story brought tears to my eyes. Of course I was sad for her—like the others I'd grown to care about her. But I also resented Don for putting me in this position, which made me hate myself even more. I was trapped. I could either leave—a person too weak and selfish to stand by his boyfriend when he most needs him—or stay and risk falling out of the love and affection I'd developed for Don. Obviously I stuck it out. I knew it couldn't go on forever. To be blunt, Mimi's days were numbered, so there'd be a natural end to this hell we were all living.

Well. The end came sooner than any of us had expected. It was August. In a couple of months, it would be Don's and my one-year anniversary. We'd gotten a little better at carving out time for ourselves to be a couple. We planned and took weekend trips. We even talked about getting a dog.

A bunch of us made a plan to get together. We hadn't all socialized without Mimi for many weeks. In a restaurant, talking, after having just seen Woody Allen's *Manhattan Murder Mystery*, we were all buzzing about the film—and speculating about crimes that could be committed right under our noses.

"That could be Mimi, for all we know," Don's sister, Amy, teased.

"Hey. You know she has a gun," Susan remembered.

"Really? Why?" I asked.

"It's an antique or something. Her dad gave it to her," Don said.

"So. Why bring that up? You think she'd ever kill someone? Or herself?" Our friend Ann, a crime writer, was taking copious notes.

"No. But. You know. That movie got me thinking. You don't really know what goes on behind someone's closed door," Susan added.

"Hey. What's Mimi's nurse like?" Ann asked.

"I don't know," Don said casually.

"What do you mean? I thought you hired her."

"No. You hired her."

"I talked to a nurse once over the phone, but never again . . ."

"But Don, you've spoken with her doctors . . . ?" He shook his head. We were all shocked. Because we had all witnessed how Mimi during a particularly needy spell would tell Don how the clinical trial wasn't working and how her doctors wanted to meet him. She'd tell us all about them. One was named Nigel, and he was gay. His partner was named Omar. And she'd talk about how they really loved Mimi and were invested in her recovery. Her eyes would fill when she spoke of them. Don felt bad, but he could never meet her doctors.

"That's not my job," he'd explain. Mimi had to be the boss of her own treatment. We all knew this was the rule we were following. But we remembered seeing two Polaroid photos of her doctors on Don's bulletin board.

"Mimi took those pictures. She gave them to me. So I put them up."

"Right," one of us said. "But wait, have any of us ever *seen* a doctor or a nurse or *any* health care professional of hers in the past two years?" Blink. Blink. We were stunned. All of us.

That night, each of us made a different phone call we would have thought unimaginable. One of us called her mother. Someone else tried her doctors. I called the hospital to see if I could talk them into telling me if Mimi was in their patient database.

"Try Mirabelle," I asked them frantically. "Or Mira? Or M.?" But the search came up empty. She had never been a patient of any doctor at UCLA Medical Center.

It was all a lie. Everything. There was no cancer. She was not dying. It was a con. And she'd kept it up for over two years! She was a genius, really. And fearless. A bold, fearless, needy, sociopathological, and butt-ugly genius.

The year Don took Mimi to Lourdes, Mimi's mother took her to the airport and hung out until it was time for them to head to their gate. Don remembers sitting in a coffee shop with Mimi and her mom. Mimi had shown up with her luggage and her backpack filled with her "medication." Her head was also shaved. Mimi had asked Don not to mention her cancer as it was destroying her mother and Mimi didn't want to upset her. So he didn't. When the truth came out, we learned how she'd simply told her mother she was going to

London to do a small role on a sci-fi movie Don was directing. How easily the lies could have been exposed! If Don had even mentioned Lourdes or his hopes for a cure, it would have been over. Or if Mom had had even the slightest clue about the kind of filmmaker Don was, she'd have known he wasn't the type to do sci-fi. It was such an enormous risk. It made me think her mother was in on it but that never proved to be true. Or maybe Mimi somehow wanted to get caught.

No. It was a fail-proof lie on her part, trading on nothing more than raw human empathy. So much so, actually, that Don's first reaction was relief—that this woman he'd come to love was not going to die. I couldn't believe it!

"*What* are you talking about? That bitch *stole* from you! From *us*! And not just money and time but your *trust*!" And of course we all knew there was some part of the lie in which we all played a role. How it fed us. Our thirst for drama. Or our need to be needed. Or in Don's case, to be a hero. But I didn't say any of those things. Because I was also grateful. That in some way the whole ordeal had actually brought us closer together. Forcing us to work so hard to connect right from the very beginning. To see what we were made of. And letting me see Don's capacity for a kind of love I hadn't even known was possible.

Had we all been living a lie? Yes and no. Mimi was lying. The details of her life were a lie. But our feelings and our ability to experience real love and compassion for her and for one another—that was all *real.* And proof to me that I was also capable of that same kind of love. And if I could take care of a sick, lying bag of shit like Mimi, maybe a kid or two wouldn't be beyond me.

Mimi did a little bit of jail time as a result of her fraud. Which felt like a little bit of redemption at the time. Needless to say, none of us ever saw Mimi again. I'm not mad anymore. Don and I are still very much together. With all the things I seemed to associate with being in love in my twenties: wedding rings, a house, a coffeemaker. And two kids. But now we know the difference between what's real and what isn't. Between actual love and a desperate desire to *be* loved. And that's what's remained after Mimi has become nothing more than a faded memory—a fat, needy, and thankfully *distant* memory with a gummy-toothed smile and full-on busted grille. Okay, maybe I'm still a *little* mad.

chapter three

What Happened in Vegas

Three months after Don and I had completed all the paperwork, classes, background checks, and home visits required to adopt a baby in California, we met our first birth mom candidate. I'll call her Samantha.

"It's her!" I remember screaming as I ran to another extension, tripping over the leg of an end table and cursing Crate & Barrel as I grabbed my throbbing toe. Hiding my pain, I picked up the phone with my best, cheery airline representative voice:

"Hi, Samantha! I'm so glad to hear from you." Don threw me a look from the kitchen. I could hear his voice in my head: *There's gay and there's* over*gay. Tone it down a notch!*

We asked a lot of questions about her life that were unrelated to her pregnancy, following the guidelines we'd been taught about talking to prospective birth moms. We knew she was talking to more than one couple and that the decision was in her hands. We wanted to make a good impression but didn't want to come off as desperate. We took notes about the name of her three-year-old son, Tye, her ex-boyfriend, and even her love of Wheat Thins. We'd been prepped by the adoption agency and our lawyer to follow up the call with a FedEx containing our birth mother letter, photos, and a short note that made reference to as many things as we could remember from our phone call. We wanted her to know we were interested in her and not just her baby. Sure, we weren't *as* interested in her as we were in adopting her baby, but we didn't think we were being dishonest. We are good listeners, after all, and polite. A few days later, Samantha called to say she wanted us to be the parents of her child. I couldn't believe it. Choking back tears, I asked Don, "Is this really happening?" My mind flashed to what felt like a hundred images: holding a baby, walking with a toddler, teaching a kid to ride a bike, reading bedtime stories, going to school plays, cheering at soccer games, helping with homework, teaching our kid to drive, dropping the kid off at college, standing side by side at the wedding . . . It was too much. I needed a bowl of cereal. Or six.

We spoke with Samantha a few more times to arrange a visit. She was coming from Las Vegas, so it was fairly easy to get her to Los Angeles. We agreed to put her up for three days so we could meet with the adoption lawyer, a social worker, and an obstetrician, and still have time for some sightseeing. She was to arrive on a Wednesday and would stay till Friday afternoon. We booked her a plane ticket and a hotel room that wound up being more expensive than we'd planned. Especially after discovering the soft, white, terry-cloth bathrobes had gone with her when she checked out. *Small price to pay*, we thought. We scheduled the appointments, got tickets to the Universal Studios theme park, and made plans to take her to dinner and a movie.

On that Wednesday morning we drove to the airport in silence. We parked, walked to the baggage area, and leaned against the wall to wait for her. Neither of us spoke for the longest time. We had been emailed one picture of her so we'd know what she looked like. But it still felt like any one of the people coming through those glass doors could have been her. I made eye contact with every single one of them as if to ask, *Are you Samantha?* There was an Indian man and a black woman and two businessmen . . . *not* Samantha. I had to distract myself to calm my nerves. I started imagining myself in each of the people coming down that escalator. One guy just getting back to L.A. after flying home to put down the family pet; another may have missed his original flight because he broke onto a set to work as an extra on a Meryl Streep movie before being caught and sent away; and a third seemed kind of nervous, like he was being picked up at the airport by a guy he'd only just met ten days before—a guy with whom he'd eventually settle down, make a home, and try to start a family. Why I was attributing my own life experiences to these complete strangers, I have no idea. But it did help mitigate the panic.

Don elbowed me; outside the glass doors, leaning against a pillar, wearing a backpack and smoking a cigarette, was Samantha. How had we missed her?

"Samantha?" I smiled at her. She looked up, cracked a smile, took one last drag, and stomped out her butt.

"They wouldn't let me smoke on the plane." She rolled her eyes. We both laughed and rolled our eyes as well, as though she'd been singled out for this injustice. Don commiserated: "The airlines are always making up crazy rules.

It's not like it used to be, that's for sure." What the hell was he talking about? Like he and she were experienced business travelers from the seventies!

She wore her hair pulled back and wasn't overly made up. This girl dressed for comfort and convenience and was a bit of a blank slate—really hard to read. But this didn't stop me from studying her for clues. She looked down a lot. Was she shy? Scared? She was definitely low-key. And quiet. Let me just say that I am *terrible* with people who are quiet and hard to read. I immediately assume they're miserable or mad at me and I overcompensate.

"Do you like Thai food? I do. We're taking you to Thai tonight. And a movie! Have I mentioned that? If you want. We're not going to force you to see *Ocean's Twelve*. How about *Dodgeball*? Does that sound good to you? Supposed to be hilarious. Maybe you'd rather not see a comedy. I get that. Right? I mean, what's so funny, anyway . . . ?" *Wham!* I felt a kick. Thank God. Don was able to make the tap dancing stop.

We had meals, went to appointments, and talked about movies we liked. We didn't talk that much about the baby, the adoption, or the fact that she was smoking two packs of cigarettes a day! I wanted to rip them from her hands. But we'd been warned through the process that we had to pick our battles, and smoking wasn't worth the fight. Most of the birth moms smoked, and the risk of low birth weight was far less grave than if the fetus was exposed to alcohol, cocaine, or crystal meth. I decided to try and let it go. Or at least act as though I had.

We learned Samantha's three-year old, Tye, was from a

previous boyfriend. We learned that her current boyfriend (the father of the baby she was carrying) was a crystal meth dealer. I was impressed with Samantha's honesty. She could have made up anything about him but didn't feel the need. She did, however, want to reassure us.

"But I have nothing to do with that part of his life," she said casually, in between sips of a milkshake. "The baby is fine."

"Right. Of course," I replied. But I registered the information in some dark notepad in my brain. Could she really have *nothing* to do with that part of his life? If my boyfriend sold, say, designer shoes, wouldn't I be lumping around the house in his samples? Would I really be able to resist the occasional employee discount? Realistically, wouldn't my closet be full? Loafers, wing tips, boots–I'd want them all! Don and I pretended not to care.

We took her to Universal. We thought she'd like the VIP tour we'd begged some friends to help us get. Samantha seemed unimpressed–numb, even, to most of what was put in her path. I wondered if it was a coping mechanism for cruel and violent things she may have lived through. I couldn't help wondering what this sweet girl must have seen in her short twenty-five years. I also wondered what those experiences might sound like in utero.

The tram slowed down as it approached the house where they shot *Psycho* and I noticed Samantha had jumped out. Don and I followed after her. She said she needed a cigarette break. Samantha was clearly impervious to Hollywood nostalgia, so we headed back to the parking garage.

The next morning we visited the obstetrician for a

checkup. He confirmed that Samantha was in her third month of pregnancy and asked to see her again in four weeks. He gave her a few boxes of prenatal vitamins and sent her off. "You got anything for me?" I asked the doctor. I wanted to do something in preparation for this baby. He smiled and made us a print of her ultrasound that Don and I stared at for about two hours when we got home.

We took Samantha to the airport, slipped her some "travel money," and promised to call her the next day. The lawyer had warned us against giving her any money, officially. It is illegal to buy a baby in California, so we were limited to pregnancy-related expenses, which would have to be documented and would likely be scrutinized closely by the courts. All financial requests were to go through his office and be paid from an escrow account we set up. But we didn't see any harm in making her feel like she was being taken care of. She texted me when she got to Vegas but that was it. She didn't return any of our calls for almost two weeks. We were convinced we'd never hear from her again. We had heard stories of birth moms who backed out of their arrangements with prospective parents or changed their minds altogether. But eventually she surfaced and assured us that everything was fine. We just had to get used to the fact that she was in control of every part of the process, down to the frequency of our contact.

Over the next few weeks, contact with Samantha was limited. We assumed this was normal. But then we started hearing from her all the time because her roommate was kicking her out of her house. She feared she was going to end up on the street. She couldn't live with her mom anymore and her boyfriend wasn't an option. I didn't ask why because I was afraid of the answer. But we also knew we couldn't let our birth mom—and by default, our child—live on the street.

I started calling residence motels and apartments in Las Vegas—on the outskirts of the Strip. We didn't want to spend a fortune but wanted to make sure she and her child had food and shelter, a cell phone, and of course, a working TV.

I found a place that allowed me to pay by the week. I'd have to call at the same time every Monday and give them my credit card number and they'd charge it for another week. Samantha asked if we could just send her the rent, but I didn't feel comfortable and again, we'd been advised against sending money directly to our birth mother. That being said, on more than one occasion Don or I would find ourselves at Western Union wiring money for "essentials." I had a sick feeling in my stomach about the whole situation, but what did I know? I assumed it was about the whole journey—about becoming a dad. Certainly women suffered a sick feeling for months of their pregnancy, so I could hardly complain. This would be *our* sick feeling. It was our first venture into open adoption, and I kept hearing I had to breathe and keep an open mind—and a bottle of Maalox handy.

We'd call. No answer. Call again. No answer. "Maybe she's out of town?" Don would offer. "With what money?" I'd ask. No way she was out of town. In my mind, she was lying facedown on the floor of her motel room surrounded by hypodermic needles.

Around this time, our lawyer called to ask if Samantha had taken her mandatory blood screening. We checked with our doctor, whose office confirmed my memory that they had *not* taken blood at her last visit. She had told the nurses she was "needle phobic." I decided to call Samantha's doctor in Las Vegas, whose number was on the proof-of-pregnancy document we'd received from the attorney.

The nurse, named Vicki, was a firm, impatient woman with a smoker's rasp who told me right off the bat she was not at liberty to discuss confidential medical records of patients. I tried to explain that I was one of the prospective adoptive dads of Samantha's unborn baby and I was looking at a proof of pregnancy issued by that office. She asked if I was calling from Los Angeles. "Yes," I replied. How it was relevant, I didn't know. She asked if I was in show business.

"Uh, yes," I answered, worried this would impact negatively her willingness to help. She asked if I was gay. I pretty much gave up any hope that she would be helping me out after that one, but it was too late to start making up stories.

"Yes. My partner and I are both adopting." Vicki's demeanor turned on a dime. As if to say *That's a horse of a different color!* She was now brighter, cheerier, and all giggles. After I agreed to read her gay son's science fiction television pilot, *she* agreed to look up Samantha's name on the computer. I felt a wave of nausea and hot-face while I waited for Vicki to come back to the phone.

"Dan?" She then sighed deeply, which I interpreted as *I've got really bad news* but which could also have been a deep drag off one of her Merit Ultra Lights. I didn't think anyone could smoke in a medical office, but it was Vegas after all.

"We haven't seen Samantha in this office for over two years," she said, knowing full well the implications of what she was saying. "What's the date on that proof of pregnancy you're holding?"

"April of this year," I told her, a little defeated.

"Well. We did one for her a few years back when she had her son, but that was the last one." She asked me to fax it to her. We stayed on the phone as the document emerged from her machine. And then: "You're looking at a cut-and-paste job, my friend," she said, with a wacky *Columbo*ish tone.

My heart sank. I mean, we knew she was pregnant, so that wasn't the issue. But her forging this medical document and lying about who knows what else did not bode well for the future of our relationship.

Coincidentally, we heard from Samantha the next day. An upcoming visit to L.A. was approaching and she needed eighty dollars to buy a suitcase. I wanted to know why she hadn't been to the doctor in two years. She didn't flinch. She said it cost fifty bucks every time she went to the doctor and she already knew she was pregnant so she didn't see the need. It was hard to argue with that logic. But then what about the blood test? I explained that she wouldn't be able to come out for the next visit until she had it.

"It's the lawyer who is insisting on it. Not us. We think it's a silly rule." We'd been told to blame all matters of procedure on the lawyer or the system or the court in order to keep our relationship as clean as possible. What also keeps the relationship clean is the birth mom not lying, not disappearing, and not forging documents so much. But nobody's perfect.

Our lawyer advised us to get out of the arrangement with Samantha as soon as he heard about the forgery. I was beyond annoyed with him for not doing any of the basic detective work *prior* to putting us together with Samantha. But his fees don't quite cover that level of investigative work. He put us together with a birth mom. The rest was up to us. In other words, you can't blame a matchmaker if the fix-up is lousy in bed. Samantha's shortcomings were clearly a result of her inexperience and modest resources. Don wanted to give Samantha the benefit of the doubt and really believed that financial hardship was what deterred her from seeing a doctor. We called her up, assured her we would cover all medical expenses, and set a time for her to see Vicki for a blood test and checkup. The night before her appointment, Don called Samantha and reiterated the importance of this doctor's visit.

"We won't be able to move ahead with the adoption if we don't get this blood test."

"I'll be there at nine a.m. sharp!" Samantha assured us.

The following morning at nine thirty, I got a call from Nurse Vicki.

"Samantha didn't show up."

I swallowed hard. "Really?"

"Please don't tell me you're surprised," she said, "because I'm not. I've seen it a million times." That didn't make me feel any better. Where was she? Why was she being so difficult? I hung up the phone. I was done. Finished. I couldn't take any more of this drama and deception.

Don called Samantha. She answered the phone, sleepily. She'd overslept! Anyone can oversleep. Right? I shrugged. Don told her to get in a cab and get to the doctor, *stat*!

An hour later, Vicki called to say that Samantha had come to the office, had a checkup, but failed to pee in the cup. She had claimed she didn't have to pee. (How many pregnant women have trouble peeing?) And to top it all off, she said she had made an appointment for a blood test at a Quest Diagnostics later that afternoon. I wasn't buying any of it anymore. I thanked Vicki for all her help and I hung up the phone.

Don and I were both now feeling we wouldn't be having a baby with Samantha but felt the need to see this thing through to the end. We needed closure. Because there was always the chance that Samantha was just nervous and scared and out of money and needed our support. She had a three-year-old son, after all. We wanted to make sure she was okay and her son was being taken care of. We had to see her in person.

We cleared the rest of the day, hopped on the next plane to Las Vegas, and rented a car when we landed. Samantha texted me directions to the Budget Motel Suites. We drove out past the Strip, past military bases and refineries. We arrived in a part of town that was worlds away from Steve Wynn and Cirque du Soleil and the money and glitz of the "What Happens in Vegas" most people know about. This part of town was just depressing. It was the dirty, tattered hem on Lady Vegas. Since I wasn't that familiar with this part of town, I'd had no idea where these "suites" were located when I was trolling online for weekly rentals. I felt a wave of guilt at having put her somewhere rundown, but frankly we were way past that now.

We pulled into the parking lot of the Budget Motel Suites and saw a family of six hanging out by the Dumpster a few feet away from the open door of their room. An old mattress had been thrown out and the kids were using it as a trampoline. It dawned on me that the use of the word "suites" in the name was a deliberate attempt to get unsuspecting losers like me to think there could be a touch of swank to the establishment. But no. There was nothing "suite" about it.

I texted Samantha, "We're here." Don and I sighed deeply, locked the car doors, and headed upstairs to room number 25, Samantha's age. We knocked, and a few seconds later Samantha answered.

"Hey guys! Come on in." Really? *Now* she's cheery and hospitable? I stepped into the room, my heart pounding, my face feeling flushed. To say I didn't feel safe is an understatement—like saying there were just a few butts in the ashtrays. With all the deception and mystery over the past few weeks, I trusted nothing. Was Samantha even her real name? I had this nagging feeling that Don and I would not make it out of Vegas alive. I fully expected Samantha to pull a knife on us, or for her boyfriend to step out of the closet or bathroom wielding a gun. I hated every second of our visit and kept practicing hitting 911 on my cell phone without looking. I was on the verge of a full-blown panic attack.

Samantha went to close the front door and I insisted we leave it open. I can't remember how I rationalized it. I know I was thinking, *So people can hear us screaming when you stab us to death!* But I said something about feeling sick from the flight and needing air, or better cell reception. She shrugged and headed back into the room.

Suddenly, the bathroom door opened and I jumped out of my skin as a short, redheaded girl named Loryn emerged.

"Nobody go in there if you don't want to die." Loryn thought this was hilarious.

I took it literally. "Oh, no thanks. I don't have to go," I said. But what I *thought* was *I don't want to die! I don't want to die!*

Loryn and Samantha started laughing hysterically. "That was my third dump today!" Loryn bragged as she lit a cigarette, ripping hard on the filter. Samantha introduced her as her homeless friend who'd been staying with her for a while. I remembered hearing about Loryn a few phone calls back. She had come into Samantha's life and basically offered herself as a personal assistant in exchange for a place to stay. Leave it to Samantha, that resourceful young schemer, to wind up with a pro bono handmaiden. Yes, I was bitter about the broken promises and forged medical documents. But I also knew she was making the best out of the limited resources she had. After all, she was taking care of a three-year-old. I just couldn't figure out how she was doing it. Where on earth did Loryn sleep? The room was small. One double bed on one wall and a kitchenette on the other. How were both girls and three-year-old Tye all staying there together? I asked.

"I know, right? And Billy sometimes too." Samantha laughed. Great. Her boyfriend and the alleged father of her baby stayed there as well! Super! My mind was racing. Shouldn't I try and get a medical history from the boyfriend too? What was his blood type? Did he have chicken pox as a kid? Flat feet? Was there mental illness, disease, or obesity in his family? Wouldn't hurt to know all that. If he was going to be around a lot, she could ask him! Wait a minute. Were they having sex here too? Of course I knew straight couples have sex throughout pregnancies. But the thought of her drug-dealer boyfriend taking her to Pound Town in front of our potential child was, let's just say, out of my comfort zone.

"Where is Billy now?" I asked, trying not to sound nervous.

"At work," Samantha answered a little too quickly. Work? I had a flash of her boyfriend in a busy office somewhere with a receptionist answering wildly flashing phones. "You've reached Tweak Time, please hold. Tweak Time, hold please. Tweak Time? . . . No, Billy's doing another line at the moment, can I take a message?" I knew not to ask any more questions.

Don quickly moved into cleaning mode. "Do you have everything you need, sweetie? Maybe we should make a Target run." There is nothing Don loves more than going to Target, filling a shopping cart with mops and towels and sprays and polishes, and taking on a huge cleaning project. And that's exactly what we did. Eventually. But first things first:

"We should get to Quest before they close," I said. There was no way we would miss this appointment. Even if it killed me. And it probably would. Or Billy would. Or Loryn. Or more likely I'd die of a heart attack from the stress.

We all piled into the rental car and drove along this strange, industrial part of Las Vegas I never knew existed. We finally pulled into a large brown cement building with an enormous QUEST sign on top. From the look of the sign, you'd think there were dancing girls and video poker inside the building. The parking lot was huge. Clearly, blood tests were in hot demand in this part of the world.

I walked with Samantha up to the first available window (there were eight) and helped her with the paperwork. Finally she was called and I watched as she was taken into one of the lab rooms. Confident that she couldn't weasel out of the test again, I joined Don and Loryn outside for about fifteen minutes, waiting for Samantha to emerge from the building.

Samantha came out and lit a cigarette. It was done. I breathed a huge sigh of relief. No matter what happened now, that blood was safely in a tube awaiting analysis. It felt like the entire future of my family was inside that tube.

Don and I knew we wouldn't hear the results of the blood test for a few days, so there was nothing for us to do now but wait. It was awkward with Samantha. On the one hand, we wanted to go home right then and there. On the other hand, this young woman and her gal Friday/friend/accomplice had so little, we didn't want to leave them without giving them a hot meal, some supplies, and a quick dry-mop. We both wanted to make our visit about more than testing Samantha's blood. So there was only one logical thing to do: we went to Olive Garden.

We were being seated at a booth just a few yards from the pasta buffet. A basket of breadsticks and rolls immediately arrived on the table. Loryn emptied the basket into her purse. "Anyone mind?" We shook our heads. Don asked for another basket, and this time, Samantha pocketed the loot. She then slid out of the booth and headed outside for a cigarette. Don told Loryn to hang back and wait with him to order some appetizers as he signaled for me to go after Samantha and keep her company. Which I did.

I got outside and bummed one of Samantha's cigarettes. It had been a while since I'd smoked. The Newport 100's

Menthol burned my lungs—and possibly every other one of my internal organs. But I rallied. The smoking ritual really helped cut the tension, which was already thick.

"I've never been to Olive Garden before," I said. Samantha looked at me. She was quiet. She took another drag off her cigarette and exhaled. "You know, secondhand meth smoke can sometimes show in the blood."

"What?" I asked. But I'd heard her. Crystal clear, so to speak. This was her way of admitting she'd been using drugs. Whatever attachment I still had to Samantha, my belief that she was our ticket to becoming parents was now hopelessly broken.

"I tried to tell Billy not to be tweakin' around me and Tye, but he doesn't always listen."

I nodded. What does one say to that? "Oh, men," I said weakly. We went back inside. We ate. I tried to tell Don *It's over* with my eyes. But it wasn't until we were alone in the car, after we'd stopped at Target for supplies and gone back to the "suite" to help tidy up, that we finally said goodbye to Samantha.

Don and I had missed the last flight back to Los Angeles. I pulled into the Stratosphere, where I was able to get us a sixty-nine-dollar room for the night. It was depressing. We lay in bed, wide awake, the prospect of becoming fathers so much farther away than when we'd arrived. I wanted to cry. Sad from the loss, yes, but also sad that we felt such relief.

Two days later, we heard from the doctor that her blood tested positive for methamphetamine. Duh. Two days after that we called Samantha. We got her voicemail. Don left her a message:

"Samantha, it's Don. Look, we heard about the blood test results. And we want you to know that we really care about you and want only good things for you and Tye. But with all of the deception and miscommunications and now the blood test—this isn't the way Danny and I want to start our family. We hope you understand. We will always wish only the best for you and Tye."

I sighed deeply. Now it really was over. I was overcome with emotion, wondering if we had just walked away from our last opportunity at fatherhood. While we felt enormous relief on the one hand, it was tinged with the fear that we just weren't tough enough to handle how difficult it really is to start a family.

Two months later we got the call from Monica, the woman who would become the birth mother of our two kids. Four months after that, Don got an email from Samantha, who wanted him to know that she was doing well and that her baby boy wound up with a couple of nice guys from San Diego. We were so glad. Some of these girls are really committed to the gays. I guess good grooming habits and a taste for Broadway musicals aren't the only advantage.

I'm not that spiritual a person. But I do believe the universe has a curiously powerful way of working in concert with fate or destiny or whatever to put people where they're supposed to be. Or if it's not predestined, then let's just say life has a way of forcing us to push past our fear—and the burning of a menthol cigarette and the smell of some homeless handmaiden's poop—to give us the strength and clarity to allow a *new* opportunity to become the *right* one. And you know, Nurse Vicki's son's sci-fi script? It wasn't half-bad.

chapter four

Who Knew?

We're in the waiting room of our ob-gyn in November of 2004. Don and I are so eager to find out the sex of our first child we can hardly sit. But we do, sandwiched with our birth mom, Monica, in a room filled with pregnant women and no other men. I'm nervous. So is she. She's chewed up most of the French manicure we treated her to a few days ago. She stands up and looks at me. "Do we have time?" she asks me. Don stays to fill out paperwork while I take her outside. I notice how much she's actually showing when we get to the curb for her quarter-hour cigarette break. Several people give her dirty looks as she lights up. She knows full well why she's getting this rebel attention. She loves it. She's on her third drag when Don calls me on my cell. She rolls her eyes and puts the cigarette out on the arm of her jacket, pocketing the "halfie" for later.

Don and I stand next to each other, staring at the ultrasound machine while our doctor rubs the sensor over her belly. We hear that echoey, futuristic, submarine-sounding heartbeat and my eyes well up. The sound is so reflective of how I'm feeling: *wow-wow-wow-wow-wow. Holy shit!* I think, *There really is a baby in there?* The doctor turns to Monica.

"You want to know the sex?" She looks up at us. "Ask them. They're the ones you gotta ask." We nod. It's a girl.

We were so excited. A girl! It was going to be so much fun! Girls seemed, at least to us, the better option for first-time parents. We assumed they'd be easier and sweeter and less likely to want us to play something horrible with them like football or smear-the-queer. Girls would be—well, more girly. I was down with that. I was already a bit on the girly side, and Don? Forget it. A kid asks him to play ball and he's likely to say, "Only if I get to be Cinderella!" With a girl, we'd get to shop for dresses and play with Barbies and twist her hair into different braids and buns and do's. Girls were made of sugar and spice and everything nice. But as it turns out there was one thing girls have that we were less experienced with. That would be the, you know, "down there" area.

Let me be clear: I've never been one of those gays who have anything against vaginas per se. I was just never particularly interested in them. Seeing them. Touching them. I didn't ever really get them. I mean, one or two, maybe. But it was just a phase because I just didn't *get* them. So many intricate folds. Canals. Wrinkles. So many places to get lost or get things lost in. Even as a kid, a girl's "down there" was just plain baffling.

When I was seven Natalie Rovner and I had a sleepover campout one summer in her backyard. She convinced me to show her my penis and I'd get to see her vagina. I would "get to," her exact words. It was supposed to be the big incentive for exposing my junk. I say Natalie made out like a bandit in the deal. I remember thinking, *Geez. Couldn't I see her vagina* and *also get a Snickers?* But I knew I was supposed to care, so my pants were around my ankles before she could say, "Don't ever tell a soul." I flashed her. She flashed me. I zipped up my pants and my sleeping bag and went to sleep. I immediately felt guilty. At the time I thought I'd done something horribly wrong.

But in hindsight, I think my guilt had more to do with knowing I was supposed to relish the opportunity to see Natalie's vajayjay and I so didn't. Something was wrong with me. Clearly. I was ashamed at my inability to pray at the altar of Miss Mary's snatch. Natalie could've offered to show me a frog and I'd have been more excited. And I was scared of frogs. As it turns out, I was much more scared of beavers.

As I hit puberty, my relationship to the female anatomy got even more complicated. I remember when I was twelve or thirteen my best friend Philip and I would get our parents to let us go from the suburbs into New York City alone on the train to have lunch or see a movie or whatever. Well. I don't know what my parents thought "whatever" was, but I can tell you it was all about getting the newsstand guys to sell us porn.

We planned each trip with precision and detail—the way one might pull off a heist at, say, Van Cleef & Arpels, complete with fake IDs and disguises. Philip would wear a hat. I'd wear a jacket and tie. And smoke. Well, I'd try. I'd pull a few half butts out of the ashtray of my dad's Buick Skylark and save them for such missions. According to our plan, we'd try and get the newsstand guys to think we were commuters: *Oh, here come a couple of Dapper Dans just off work at the firm and on their way to Grand Central to catch the 7:25 back home to their wives.* I looked thirteen well into my twenties; when

I was thirteen, I looked nine. I was short. Had rosy cheeks. Lots of freckles. Philip looked maybe a year older but he had braces, the perfect touch—if we wanted to look like we were on our way to our bar mitzvahs. We thought we looked at least twenty.

Suffice it to say, we *always* got the porn. I'm sure the vendors laughed, but hey, a sale is a sale, right? Not only that, but we'd often stop at the Grey Car Lounge at Grand Central Station for a cocktail before we boarded our train home to our "wives." I'm sure we were completely inconspicuous: two pubescent nerds in hats and jackets ordering Amaretto Sours with extra cherries. Yeah, right.

It was on one of these secret missions to New York where I got my first close-up view of an actual lady vagina. And I'm not talking about some "tasteful" arty spread in *Playboy* with their modesty poses and dainty trimming. No. These publications, like one called *ClimaXXX*, were considered hard-core, so the women were always spread-eagle, with long painted fingernails helping to lead the way. And naked guys too . . . which was clearly the *real* motivation behind the pleading looks to vendors on these long, convoluted treks into the city.

We'd get on the train and look for two seats together as far away from other commuters as possible. The magazines were in a paper bag we'd put behind one of our backs. We'd sit quietly as the train started moving. We wouldn't even look at each other. This was all part of the routine. We'd pretend to be two commuters who didn't know each other, heading home after work. It would take eight minutes for the train to come out of the long tunnel of Grand Central Station and into daylight. The conductor would always take our tickets just before the first stop at 125th Street. After the doors closed, we knew we had a good long stretch with no chance of anyone coming by.

We'd slouch really low in our seats and slide a magazine out of the paper bag. Philip would flip through the whole thing fast as sort of a preview. Then we'd go through it again, more slowly, to analyze the photos. That's when I saw it: my first grown-up vagina. I looked at Philip to see what he thought. I remember he seemed like he'd seen it all before. I couldn't hide the fact I hadn't.

"Where do they pee? Where's the hole? Do you see a hole? There's no hole!" I was desperate to understand.

"Stop saying 'hole,'" he said, before taking me through the ins and outs (so to speak) of the female anatomy. He was suspiciously confident in explaining what he himself didn't understand. Because to us, they were like the mouths of caves. One even seemed to be in 3D—a coral reef, glistening with sea life.

"Oh my God!" I said once, a little too loudly on a particularly crowded train. "That looks like it could stick to the shower wall like a shampoo caddy." We both burst out laughing. Not surprisingly, we are both now married to *men*.

For so many of our peers, gaining access to a vagina was a full-time preoccupation. Guys would talk for hours, speculating about rolling around with Erica or Debbie or Nancy or that girl, I think her name was Sapna—a buxom Indian girl who had her first period during a third-period health class all about periods. Sapna is probably a drug addict now. Some things you don't recover from.

I, on the other hand, didn't give the topic a second

thought. I managed without too much difficulty to get through high school and most of college avoiding vaginas altogether. No, during that time my attention was focused on the penis. Mine and those of anyone who'd show me theirs. There were only three:

1. Johnny Mancuso, who stepped back from a urinal to show me how he could pee the letters of his name.
2. Seth Feingold, the lead in our school play who pulled me into the bathroom to show me his "anaconda."
3. And finally, Rick, the drummer guy I met during my short stint in marching band, who dared me to show him mine but, when I refused, settled for showing me his. Then he spent the rest of the semester inviting me over for a sleepover. I politely declined. Most of the time.

It wasn't until I got to college that I had my first experience with an actual, real-life, full-grown vagina. And let me tell you, it didn't last more than twenty-two seconds. I know because I counted to myself.

One, two, three . . . Hmm. That's kind of odd. It's so warm . . . seven, eight . . . and bristly. And, twelve, thirteen . . . wait a minute, what? *Fifteen, sixteen . . . It's* wet! *Nineteen, oh my* God! *Is that—? Twenty . . . No. Okay. I can't do this . . . Twenty-one, twenty-two.* I was out. I made some excuse about study group and took off in the direction of *not* the vagina. Who knew it would be so wet?

Despite my head-for-the-hills reaction, a few years later I landed my first real girlfriend. I'll call her Nora. She was two years younger but not a virgin. I of course still was. Within a few weeks Nora started the subtle pressure for us to "do it." I can't imagine why my lack of interest in doing "it" or anything else physical wasn't a red flag. Trying to turn her off became my mission. I wouldn't make any eye contact. I'd give monosyllabic answers to her questions and I'd try to avoid all body contact. But for some reason she took my apathy as a challenge. I'd sit next to her on the couch and we'd turn on the TV. Despite the fact I had no idea what we were watching, I'd appear fully engrossed to cool down the nineteen-year-old coed sitting shoulder to shoulder with me, kissing my neck and nibbling my ear. *Freeze and maybe she'll stop. Play dead and maybe she won't attack.*

There came a point where I couldn't keep the charade going. I knew in my heart that I had to shit or get off the pot. If I wouldn't finally jump in and start having some of the sex, I'd risk losing Nora, whom I'd actually grown to love. But worse than that, it would confirm a fear I'd had since childhood: that I was, in fact, gay. It was a fear I'd promised myself would never be realized or I'd commit suicide. That's right. Having sex with Nora had become a matter of life and death.

Nora had long, dark hair, a great body—at least in the eyes of someone who couldn't have cared less—and was about my height. She had a sweet smile and loved to laugh. Particularly at everything I said. She came from a Seattle family with a lot of money. As a result, Nora was the only freshman at Vassar who drove a fully loaded, souped-up BMW with a phone in it. Nothing was cooler. Except for the long weekend in

Manhattan we spent during one spring break. Her dad was owed a favor or two by the owners of a fancy hotel on Central Park, so our whole stay was complimentary. I was stunned. A beautiful room. Bathrobes we got to keep. Room service. And what about the fact that Warren Beatty was also staying in the hotel? That did it for me. Here was Hollywood's most notorious playboy staying in the suite right above ours! If he was getting laid, for fuck's sake, so would I!

We came back to the hotel after a day of sightseeing, Broadway shows, and shopping. Jeez, I was so gay you could see it from space. You could, but we didn't. We walked into the lobby and I put my hand on the small of her back, feeling every bit the role of "the boyfriend." We got into the elevator and my stomach started doing flips. She smiled at me and I at her. It's like we both knew. I started to run a million excuses in my head to talk myself out of what I had determined to do: *I don't want to be late for* Dreamgirls. *What if someone hears and kicks us out of the hotel? We ate Indian for lunch, risky choice for lovemaking, no?* But I was climbing the steps on the high dive and I really didn't want to turn back. It was time to just walk to the edge and jump.

Nora threw her bags on the floor and I just went for it. I picked her up and threw her on the bed. In a matter of seconds, we were both naked. While we were making out, Nora led my hand down, you know, there. Thank God, because my hand wasn't going to go there by itself. It was lifeless and limp—like the victim of some self-induced stroke. But luckily, it was the only part of me that was limp.

Yes, gay guys can get erections when we are with women. We're still men, after all. It doesn't take much. A piece of fruit.

A bus seat. A hat. The drop of that hat. And the mechanics of it all? Exactly the same. Tab A goes into Slot B just like it does for everyone else. Tab A just liked to fool around with *Tab* B instead.

After a few minutes, she felt me against her and guided me to where I was supposed to be. I remember being surprised at how unremarkable it was. My mind was racing: *You're doing it! You're having sex!* Then, *Huh. Is this it? This right here is what having sex feels like? Man. What the hell is the big deal?*

Afterward, we showered and had dinner and I was on top of the world. I did it! I did it! I had sex with my girlfriend in a five-star hotel just like Warren Beatty a floor or two away. I'm a man among men. A man's man . . . a *straight* man.

It was March of 1986. I had been keeping a journal since the beginning of the previous semester, which I'd spent at the Eugene O'Neill Theater Center studying theater, dance, and puppetry. (Why didn't they just call it the Center for Gay Studies?) Here's the entry in my journal after that fateful night:

March 11, 1986. New York City.

Well, it happened! Tonight I am a man. That sounds so stupid. But it's true. Tonight, Nora and I finally did "it." We had sex. I'm no longer a virgin. I can't believe it. After all this time. And all the nervousness. And all the worry. I have to admit—it was over so fast. ~~*And I didn't really like*~~ *It didn't really feel the way I thought it would feel. Kind of no big deal. Anyway. I'm so happy! Because now there's no going back! Nobody can take it away from me. I just hope she doesn't want to do it all the time now.*

Before Nora had the chance to even hint at doing it again, the following night I was feeling pretty cocky. *Let's do it again,* I thought. *Why not? Really seal the deal.* So we got ready for bed, slid into the million-thread-count sheets, and I immediately rolled on top of her. Again, she guided me. Only this time, I felt something different.

Wait a minute! What's happening here? I thought. I felt a tiny bit of pressure and then most definitely the warm tight wetness that could mean only one thing: I was inside her. Again, my mind was racing.

This was *nothing* like the night before. So what the hell had that been?

It turned out I hadn't lost my virginity to Nora on that first night. I lost it to the side of her leg and maybe some rolled-up sheets. Why she didn't *tell* me I had taken a wrong turn or failed to yield at the intersection, I can't for the life of me figure out. Was she trying to protect me from embarrassment? The second night was unmistakable. I was most definitely inside another human being for the first time in my life. And a woman, at that! It's interesting the way biology or evolution or whatever set it up so the male could pretty much have a positive sexual experience with anything warm enough, wet enough, and tight enough. Not to minimize the role of attraction, seduction, and dare I say, love, that add the *sexy* factor to the game. But speaking strictly of the act of intercourse itself, a hole is a hole. And it wouldn't be fair to say I didn't enjoy it.

Nora and I continued to have a moderately healthy sex life for the next few months. And by "healthy" I mean we had one, but I wasn't into it. And she knew it. We'd fight all the time. I wanted her to break up with me. She'd burst into tears in the campus student center and scream, "You treat me like a whore!"

True, I was a shitty boyfriend, no doubt—and a lousy lay. But the one thing I guarantee I was *not* doing? Treating her like a whore. If anything, I would have paid cash money to *not* have sex with her. While a small part of me was pretty proud of my ability to sell the straight guy story, I felt terrible about how Nora was feeling. But I couldn't admit to myself that it was a problem on my end. I knew it was over. But I didn't want to admit to the reason—not yet. By the end of the school year, it was obvious that neither of us was happy. I had mustered enough courage and respect for Nora and myself to tell her I thought I wasn't equipped to be a boyfriend to her and that we should just be friends. Nora cried. No doubt some of those tears were from relief. She could stop fighting so hard. And so could I.

Years later I tracked down Nora and the few other women I'd dated over the years just to let them know, "It wasn't you." I was relieved to see how most were already involved with other people, grateful for the honesty, and almost bored by the information. It was something I felt I needed to do—part of my journey.

It took a few more years after college before I was able to admit to the world, my family, and myself that what I really wanted was *anything but* a vagina. I was gay. No other way to frame it. And the people who knew and loved me were relieved to hear it from me—but not surprised.

• • •

From then until I became a father, I had no real connection to or contact with vaginas to speak of, although most of my friends have them. But then, as fate would have it, I was blessed with a daughter. And as fate would have it, she has one too. I can't close the case file on the vagina just yet. It was clear there was much more for me to do vis-à-vis the vajayjay.

Eliza comes up to me out of the blue one day and tells me she has ten babies in her tummy.

"Oh wow," I say, "that's a lot. Who's going to help you take care of all those kids?" Yes. Even in this childish game of make-believe, Daddy's concerned about child care and the cost of getting all those kids fed.

"You are, Daddy!" Eliza says. "And Papi too! But they're not going to come out until I'm growned up." Ahhh. Excellent plan.

"Does it hurt?" Eliza wonders if the birthing process hurts. Jesus. I don't want to scare her. But I also don't want to lie.

"Um, a little, I think, sweetie. But I'm a boy. So I've never had that experience. Only girls can have babies."

She rolls her eyes. "I know that." She then wonders aloud how the babies can squeeze out of the belly button.

"No, honey." I laugh. "The babies come out of a woman's vagina." Eliza goes white. She blinks. And then again. She can't quite believe it. And really, who can? It's clearly not been thought through. Some evolutionary brainstorming session probably led to a whole bunch of crazy ideas and somehow this one made it through.

"No!" She thinks I'm kidding. I assure her it's true. She spends the rest of the week asking every woman she knows if they had a baby out their vagina and if it hurt. Eliza announces proudly, "I want medicine so it won't hurt." Take a note: Eliza opts for the epidural. Sounds good. Get that request in early.

Ever since that birth chat, I notice Eliza looking at her vagina more. Touching it. Exploring it. I secretly wish she wouldn't. And I wish even more that I didn't wish she wouldn't.

"I like taking off my underwear, Daddy!" she announced the other day. I flash forward ten years and pray to *God* she's not saying the same thing to some guy in his parents' Volvo hatchback on level P3 of a mall parking structure, after seeing *Fame* for the third time. Oh wait. That was me.

I know I have to help my daughter learn to drive her vagina responsibly. Eventually. You know, so she comes to realize the respect she should have for her hoo-hoo. And maybe by then her daddy will too. Or at least have evolved enough to stop calling it a "hoo-hoo." But what's the hurry? Don wants grandkids early, so he may have a different approach. For right now? I'd be happy to put police tape over the area and scoot her in another direction: *Move along now, nothing to see here.*

chapter five

Aunt Cuckoo

I met my friend Julie (not her real name) at the same game of Celebrity where I met Don in 1992. She had worked with him on some eighties television show about a hospital staff that spent a lot of time disrobing. They jokingly referred to the show as *High Hair and Underpants.* Don and I were forced by Linda, who set us up, to be a team during the first round of Celebrity. I remember feeling like an idiot when I couldn't guess the clues for Boutros Boutros-Ghali and Rula Lenska, and Julie very sweetly came to my rescue. I liked her right away. She was funny, smart, and irreverent. And she immediately made me feel comfortable when I was clearly an outsider. At the time, she sort of worked the grunge thing before anyone else had—and then worked it way past its expiration date. She wore a lot of hats. I teased her that one of them looked like a colander and she laughed. We both did. That was it. We were friends. Pretty soon we were talking every day, laughing, gossiping.

Many years later, Julie came down with a pesky case of depression. She retreated, closed herself off, and rarely left the house. Occasionally, though, she would agree to meet at a

Sizzler or an Applebee's, where she wouldn't run into anyone she knew.

A short time after my fateful call to Don from the film set in Italy, Julie and I met for one of her trademark clandestine dinners deep in the Valley, where you can't throw a rock without hitting a blooming onion—or a meth lab. I told her the good news: Don and I were thinking of adopting! Now, there's a reason people like being bearers of good news. The response is always predictably great: a squeal of delight, a big hug, a "hip, hip hooray!"

But Julie distinguished herself from everyone else by her reaction: she tried to talk me out of it. "Your life will never be the same." "You'll never sleep soundly again." "You can kiss your relationship goodbye." "Do you know how fast people age once they have kids?" "Old and fat. Get used to those words." "You don't have a house for kids. Your floors are limestone. Your stairs are treacherous. Try recovering from a dead baby."

And then, as though she still saw a tiny bit of life, in my still and lifeless body, one more: "It's not just babies who die, mister. You know how many people die during childbirth?"

I managed to croak out, "But we're going to adopt."

She was obstinate: "Google it!"

I didn't quite know what to say. I just started laughing. Nervously. The way you laugh when you think, *Oh dear, am I in a car, miles from anywhere with a crazy person who might at any moment whip out an axe and hack away at my neck in what will undoubtedly become an urban legend told by frightened campers zipped into sleeping bags?*

We had limited contact with Julie over the next couple of years. A few short visits to see the baby. Once with a gift:

a pink, stuffed elephant in disco pants, seriously, which I decided to take as a dig. And that was it. Until Eliza was almost two and having a procedure to repair a hole in her heart called an atrial septal defect (ASD).

Julie fought back her demons and came out of hibernation to join us at the hospital. She was there along with many of our other close friends, by our side, all day and night. The procedure involved inserting a device called an Aplatzer Septal Occluder via catheter through a vein in her leg, as they do with stents. The operation was supposed to take only ninety minutes. But due to complications it took an unbearable four hours. To say nothing prepares you for parenthood is a cliché. But when you are watching your twenty-month-old baby girl on a gurney, clutching her stuffed kitten with one arm, the other plugged with an IV as she's wheeled back into an operating room—that's a feeling of powerlessness and sheer panic that would deter anyone from becoming a parent in the first place. It was in that moment I wondered if Julie hadn't been right. It's one thing to paint a nursery or shop for diaper bags to prepare for the arrival of your baby. But what about all the variables you could never predict? Having a kid had brought us to this free-falling moment for which there seemed to be no safety net. Our friends, and Julie in particular, showered us with reassuring optimism and confidence. And we had complete faith in our pediatric cardiologist. But the *what-ifs* really started to kick in at hour two. It was particularly hard on Don, who was panicked over the possibility the procedure might not work and we'd be faced with open-heart surgery. At that point, I managed to summon an inner strength I hadn't realized I had. I looked Don squarely in the eyes and reminded him our little girl was depending on us to be pillars of courage and reassurance.

Eliza's procedure was a success. The next day, we took her home, and by the third day, surprisingly she had pretty much recovered. We were nervous, of course, but Eliza seemed to have an unexpected surge in energy almost immediately. She had blossomed into a different kid! Poor thing, her heart had been working overtime for nearly two years.

Something changed with Julie too and she was suddenly much more present in our lives. We had never really talked about the time before the surgery, but afterward she started coming around once a week to spend time with Eliza and later with Jonah too. It was awkward at first. She was uncharacteristically chipper and energetic and, let's just say, had no concept of an "inside voice." She'd whip Eliza around in the air and they'd both scream with laughter.

Though the doctors said it was fine, we weren't so much into the roughhousing right after heart surgery. We liked smooth-housing or, better yet, *no*-housing, like: "Hey, Eliza? You know what would be fun? Let's sit *very* still and try to listen for heartbeats. *Your* heartbeat, actually. Do you have a heartbeat, darling? Please say yes . . ."

But that wasn't how Julie played it. Julie had a funsy, Bozo the Clown–type energy. We were sure it was too much for our delicate little flower. But Eliza loved it. Julie had a way with Eliza that was irresistible. She managed to be so magically intuitive, focused, and yes, fun! We had a real-life Barney playing with our daughter—and not just when she wore purple. They also developed delicious secrets, which the kids loved. Me? Not so much. I snuck in on them once watching TV and eating cookies out of a box. Julie was whispering, "We don't have to tell Papi or Daddy about every cookie we eat, do we?"

Oh, *yes you do!* But when Eliza was with Julie, there were no rules, no bedtimes, no limits. Julie was her irresistibly wild-eyed, energetic, and fun-loving aunt. We affectionately called her Aunt Cuckoo.

Even a year after the operation, we were still Aunt Cuckoo's bitches. Every morning as we'd drive Eliza to school, she'd start asking to call Julie as we backed down the driveway. I would dial her on speakerphone.

Ring. Ring. Eliza's face would beam with anticipation. *Ring. Ring.* No answer. I'd start to panic.

"Pick up the phone, Aunt Cuckoo!" *Ring. Ring.* Eliza would look at me, worried. Then, thank God, the click.

"Hello?"

I could breathe again.

Eliza would beam from ear to ear. "Hi . . ." she'd say, suddenly shy, as though she were talking to Lady Gaga, or Anderson Cooper or okay, no, *Cinderella.*

Julie would always say the same thing: "It's peanut butter jelly time!"

Eliza would laugh. Highlight of her day. I couldn't help but resent Aunt Cuckoo for it. And Eliza. Here I was, working so hard to be her parent, to love and provide for her and teach her about kindness and moderation and limits. Why didn't she like me, her own father, better than our friend, an unabashed, hedonistic, sugar and TV pusher? Oh yeah, that's why.

At especially low moments, I would try to imitate Aunt Cuckoo. "Peanut butter jelly time!" I'd sing. And my kids would just look at me. Blink. Blink. I've seen that look countless times in casting. A look that says, *Aww. Nice try. But we're gonna go a different way.*

Bedtime was no different. I'd pick up a book and three-year-old Eliza would just say, "Can we call Aunt Julie?" I'd think, *No way! It's story time.*

"No, sweetie. Aunt Julie is—is—well . . ." *No. Don't do it,* I'd think. But I couldn't help myself. "Julie is sick. Very sick." I'd hit an all-time low. Sick? Did I really want to be *that* guy?

"I mean tired, sweetie. She's sleeping, which is what you should be doing." I'd try and distract her with some tickling and tempt her with an organic, all-natural, fiber gummy bear. Didn't quite cut it.

"Sweet dreams, monkey. Tomorrow morning, Daddy is going to make pancakes in little animal shapes and—"

She'd cut me off: "Call Julie?"

"*Yes!* Fine," I'd concede. "Tomorrow you can call Julie."

Next morning, my sleeping angel's eyes peek open, blink, and her first words are *"Call Julie?" For the love of God!* What about Daddy's pancakes, huh? *What about Daddy's fucking pancakes in the shape of Daddy's broken heart?*

On the afternoons of Julie's visits, Eliza would even sit in a chair at the front door and wait for her up to an hour before she was scheduled to arrive. She wasn't waiting like that for me to get home. How did it happen? My daughter had become a crazy, stalky fan of the one person who had done everything in her power to talk me out of having a child in the first place.

Of course it is a two-way street. The kids did more for Aunt Cuckoo than any of us grown-ups could. They loved her unconditionally and made her feel important; they made her able to laugh and run and forget herself, at least for the amount of time it takes to get through *101 Dalmatians* and a dozen chocolate-chip-and-partially-hydrogenated-oil cookies. But there it is. *I* didn't do that.

I want life to be neat and predictable and safe and calm and quiet and controlled, with *no* surprises like tricky little heart defects. But Eliza herself proved how small and wrong and petty that thinking was with her big, open, generous heart. After all this time, turns out it was Daddy who had the heart defect, not Eliza. So my kids teach me what Aunt Cuckoo teaches them: that life is infinitely more fun when it's crazy and unpredictable and undisciplined and fundamentally bad for your health. And the sooner you get an Aunt Cuckoo in your life to show you that, the better.

chapter six

To Cut or Not to Cut

Don and I decided to try and adopt another baby just before Eliza's second birthday. We were conflicted about it, for sure. It was only about a month after Eliza's heart procedure—an ordeal that seemed to test the very limits of our emotional capacities. She was fully recovered. Tons more energy; she was a different kid, really. We took a little longer. I mean, every time she'd smile at us or do something cute or, you know, not dead-like, we'd squirt tears of joy.

"Did you see that? She's eating yogurt!" *Boo-hoo-hoo* . . . We were so happy with our healthy little girl and felt so complete already as a family of three, it seemed piggy to ask for a second. We tried to put all thoughts of baby number two out of our heads.

But it kept coming up. Both Don and I are close with our siblings. My sister was there for me at so many crucial moments of my life, not the least of which was the day after Eliza was born. Don escorted Monica back to Wisconsin with her one-year-old twins and I was home with a newborn. My sister dropped everything, three kids of her own, and came to my rescue for a few days. Likewise, there is no way I could've gotten through the loss of my father that same year if it weren't for my sister. We both believed Eliza deserved to have that kind of ally in her life. Even if it just meant another person with whom she could bitch about her crazy, faggy dads!

We called our lawyer and he put our names on the list. But months went by and we weren't getting any calls. "The birth mom market is drying up," our lawyer said. We couldn't imagine why. Had high school hall monitors gotten more vigilant about checking bathroom stalls? Don and I were both secretly relieved. Maybe it wasn't meant to be. People are always saying that "you wind up with the kid you're *supposed* to have." I never used to believe that "everything happens for a reason" crap, but maybe in this instance, we were supposed to have just one.

That's when the phone rang. It was around February. Monica, Eliza's then twenty-one-year-old birth mom, called us.

"You ready for a new one?" she asked me casually, as though she worked at a dealership and was calling with a friendly reminder that our lease was up.

She and her "husband" were having a hard enough time making things work with her three-year-old twins; another baby wasn't going to be possible for them. We tried to contain our joy out of respect for Monica. But she knew we were thrilled. And she was relieved. Eliza would have a sibling! There was no way we could say no.

Off we embarked on another six-month journey to prepare for baby number two. Don and I were both sort of in denial about it. I kept telling myself the reality would kick in when the baby was here. Given the year we'd had—Eliza's surgery, followed by my dad's death—it all felt like I was getting a crash course in the circle of life.

But on September 6 at around eight in the morning there was no denying it anymore. We were back in the delivery room to witness the birth of our gorgeous, eight-pound, twenty-one-inch, healthy baby boy, Jonah (the "J" from my dad Julio's name) Paul (Don's middle name) Bucatinsky (because my family was dwindling and I won at rock/paper/scissors).

This was when we began our spirited little debate over circumcision. I thought it was a foregone conclusion. Who doesn't circumcise? Other cultures. People in countries far, far away. Members of the animal kingdom. No offense. Of course, we all know anytime someone says "no offense," it's probably too late. But honestly, I'm a big fan of the animal kingdom. Except snakes, most birds, and raccoons. They're mean.

I'm Jewish. Don is Catholic. We're both circumcised and so I never gave it a second thought. But Don, a recent born-again atheist, admitted he'd always thought the practice to be barbaric and pleaded with me to leave our son's body alone. To be honest, I had, or I should say I *have*, never seen a real live uncircumcised penis. Except maybe in a porno. Not that I watch them. But I may have seen one playing in the background somewhere at someone else's house. Maybe. A very long, long time ago. And who knows, really, 'cause when they're erect they all look the same. Give or take five inches.

"It's a cultural thing. It's a Jewish tradition," I'd say.

Don argued back, "The only thing Jewish about you is you hate mayonnaise."

"What?" I asked. "What does that even mean? I *do* hate mayonnaise, but I know plenty of Jews who love it. And I'm sure plenty of non-Jews hate it." Although growing up, I did envy those kids at my school with bologna sandwiches on Wonder Bread with tons of mayonnaise, wrapped in waxed paper. We never had any of that stuff. I mean, we had turkey and ham but always on rye bread. And once in a while there'd be pastrami or tongue. Tongue! Who the hell ever thought that would make a good sandwich?

I tried to find my way back to a point: "But lots of the blond-haired *non*-Jews had white bread sandwiches that *weren't* slathered in mayo in their lunch bags. And I'd be willing to bet some of them were circumcised." Huh? I was lost. So I *know* Don was too. I brought it back: "I want our son to look like both of us."

Don wouldn't have it. "How often are we going to be comparing penises with our son? We're gay men. You want to ask the guys at Social Services who are gonna take our kids from us if *they're* circumcised? Are you looking for jail time with supervised visitation?"

"It's a health issue!" I brought out the big guns, pelting him with statistics: "Penile cancer occurs in one in six hundred men in this country but neonatal circumcision abolishes the risk. Uncircumcised boys are ten times more likely to get urinary tract infections."

He cuts me off with "Super! I bet you men with no fingers get fewer hangnails too. Let's lop those off. Or we can suck his brains out to prevent headaches."

I'd grown accustomed to our having different points of view. Believe me. Over the years we haven't always seen eye to eye. And certainly after Eliza was born. Wow. How on earth had we neglected to discuss our parenting philosophies *before* we had a child? I'm a stickler for minimal TV, healthy diet, no grazing. I'm for more government intervention and Don much less. I never thought it would come down to Democrat versus Republican in my own house. We both always voted the same. And with the bigger issues, we tend to find our way to the same page. But now the Circumcision Caucus was upon us and the differing points of view so clearly defined. We just didn't agree on them. Even though one party was so obviously right. I knew how Don felt. He knew how I felt. We were going to have to compromise. But you can hardly meet halfway with something like this. You either cut or you don't cut.

In the end, we agreed Jonah would be circumcised by the doctor in the hospital. There'd be no ceremony (no slicing open a smoked salmon after slicing our baby's foreskin). And Don, who gets queasy at the sight of a paper cut, would not be in the room with me when it happened. I'd have to be there alone. I was disappointed we wouldn't have a traditional bris. But we had found a compromise and I appreciated that.

We didn't speak of it again. I hoped it wouldn't create too much of a rift between us during this tense and uncertain time. Adoption's not without its stresses, especially during the seventy-two hours in which the birth mom still has the chance to change her mind.

As we had done with Eliza, the day after Jonah's birth Don and I took turns taking care of Monica. Each night of her hospital stay, one of us would sleep in her room. We brought her tabloids with photos of celebrities who were "just like us" and had more cellulite than she did. That always seemed to put her in a good mood. We'd also bring her favorite refreshments and movies, and we snuck her cigarettes. Making matters worse, she had always suffered a great deal of postpartum depression after having her kids. I imagine that's particularly difficult for a mom involved in an adoption plan.

The night after the birth it was my turn to sleep overnight on the pullout in Monica's room. Well, I don't know if "sleep" is an accurate term. It was more like sporadic, hour-long naps in between wheeling Monica down to the plaza for cigarette breaks.

At seven in the morning, Don showed up at the hospital. Jonah's circumcision had been scheduled for seven thirty. I looked like shit. If shit had bad hair and bags under its eyes. Don gave me a hug and walked with me to the nursery to admire our new son. Don then pulled out a cloth bag containing my father's yarmulke and a picture of both my parents.

"I thought you might want them with you while the doctor performed the bris," he said.

He called it a bris. He then handed me the prayers he had Googled and printed out. He'd also invited two of my close friends, Michael and Sylvie, both Jewish, to hold my hand through the process. And as if the universe were conspiring with all of us, the doctor and nurses agreed to break their biggest rule and allowed us all into the back of the nursery, with my camera and the picture of my parents. We made a ceremony of it after all—a ceremony that took on meaning far greater than the tip of my son's penis. Maybe the best parenting in the world, the most respected philosophies on sleep training, food schedules, TV watching, and discipline, can't beat raising a child in a home where his two parents actually love each other. And show it. At least once in a while . . .

chapter seven

Pee on the Hand, Poop on the Coat

We are all at a beach house in Cape Cod with my sister and her family. But the kids are nowhere to be found. Jonah and Eliza went off to play with their cousin about half an hour ago.

I've just loaded the car with the cooler and towels and chairs and sand shoes and floaties and goggles and pails for the day at the beach. Now I just need to add two kids to the recipe. "Guys? Where are you? Come on . . . time to go to the beach!" My calls go completely unanswered. I start looking for them in the house, upstairs, every bathroom . . . then downstairs . . . and finally I enter one of the bedrooms. There, on the bed, are my two kids, their legs over their heads, each one taking turns sniffing each other's asses. Thank *God* they were all clothed. Among all the things I imagined they could be doing, I wasn't expecting this one.

"Um . . . what are you guys doing?" I am so afraid to hear the answer.

"We're playing kitties, Daddy!" Eliza flips back up and skips over to me. "Cats sniff each other's tails as a way of saying hello." She seems so chipper.

Clearly this is a moment for some kind of parental intervention, right? But what? It's not like I've ever heard any opinions on what to do when your kids are sniffing ass. I mean, I must have missed the chapter on that one.

"All right, well . . . hurry up and get your flip-flops 'cause we're leaving for the beach." I decided to pretend I thought it was cute. Or that it didn't actually happen. That particular technique has served me well when I find myself in a parental quandary for which I'm completely unprepared.

On the subject of parental things I never thought I'd have to think about and sure as hell aren't in any parenting books, how about trying to collect a urine sample from a four-year-old girl? Eliza was complaining of pain when she pees, so the doctors asked for a urine sample. For my entire life, a urine sample has been among the easiest things for a guy to provide. But here I was, on my knees, holding a cup between my daughter's legs as she sat on the toilet. Where the hell do I hold the cup? It's a wild guess, really. I try to center my hand in the general vicinity but I have no real idea where the stream will come from. Ope! There it is, all over my hand . . . and not in the cup. Now what? She's going to have to drink six cups of water and we'll have to try this all again. Are you kidding me? Has nobody come up with a contraption to get a girl's pee into that tiny cup with more precision and ease? Sure, when she's a little older, she can do it herself. But she's four. She doesn't want to hold the cup.

Oh. And how about the six weeks after a circumcision? Does anyone actually prep you for the fact that you have to pull your poor son's foreskin back every time you change him, and slather the area with Vaseline to avoid a hideous phenomenon known as "reattachment"? That's right. If you don't lube it up three or four times a day, the foreskin can *reattach* and you have to bring the poor baby back to *detach* it again. I may be a little paranoid and somewhat defensive, but there's no contest for the mortification the first time our nanny walked over to me, a gay man, while I was changing Jonah. She looked at me like I had lost my mind and managed to croak out, "Danny? What are you doing?"

"Oh, well, there's something called reattachment and it's, um—there's really only one way to avoid—well . . ." You know how much *not* fun it is to explain to the nannies and babysitters how you want them to give your kid a handie every time they change him? How come nobody told me about that?

Or how about the time Eliza was only a year old and I brought her to someone's holiday open house. The place was packed. And so was my daughter. The poor thing hadn't pooped in three days. I had her in the Bjorn as I waited in the eggnog line when she started contorting her little face. Her cheeks got so red, it made the suit on the Santa-for-hire look washed out.

I took Eliza upstairs and laid her on the bed after clearing an area on the mountain of coats. I prepared to change her diaper, only the diaper was clean! My poor kid was screaming as I saw a shiny head of poop at a complete standstill at the opening of her tush. She was crowning! But that baby wasn't coming out. No traffic moving in either direction. I had no idea what my next move was supposed to be. Forgive me for not adding that to the list of things I Googled when I knew we were expecting a baby: "removing a zeppelin-sized turd out an infant's ass." *Search!*

I left Eliza on the bed surrounded by coats and sneaked into the bathroom, where I combed the medicine chests for some Vaseline. Finally, I found some Preparation H. I squinted at the label to see if it would kill a kid to have a dab. After all, the stuff was supposed to "shrink swelling" and that seemed appropriate in this situation. I slathered it on my finger and went carefully into the cave to ease out the boulder. First one side. Then the other. And then *pow.* That thing flew out and onto someone's Patagonia down jacket. I managed to clean it and the baby and replace her diaper with a clean one. At long last, it looked like the weight of the world was off her—okay, well, out of her. But really? I could've done without adding that whole experience to my life wallet.

I received no fewer than six copies of *What to Expect When You're Expecting* in baby gift baskets when the kids were born. The book is great but, as it turns out, somewhat limited. It was certainly of no use one bath time when Jonah was only one. Where's the book *What to Expect Will Float to the Surface When Your Kid Sneezes During Bath Time*?

chapter eight

Bam Bam

Seeing Jonah, all three feet, forty-five pounds of him, with his little tough guy swagger, I am often transported back to the terror and panic of junior high school. The strident squeaks of kids' sneakers running toward class, and the slamming of lockers. And the slamming of *me* inside those lockers. I still carry a lot of anxiety and insecurity from those days. For some reason, I'm fixated on the weeklong wrestling unit we had in gym class.

The sight of those smelly blue wrestling mats lined up on the floor would put me in a state of "teacher, I want to go home." We'd be paired up in size order. I was a shrimp and would always be thrown onto the mat with skinny, cross-eyed Warren Fink. He always seemed particularly bored by my tactic of dancing around the mat, avoiding contact. Eventually I would tire and Warren would come at me with a surge of focus and intensity, his crossed eye drifting even farther toward the bridge of his nose. He'd bite his lip and dive toward me. All the other guys would surround the mat screaming, "Kill him!" I'd look up at them and explain, "I'm trying!" But inevitably they'd scream back, "Not you! Warren! Kill *him*!" Meaning *me*. Those guys, for some reason, wanted him to kill me. "Those" guys.

They all had a particular strut I was never able to perfect. A little bowlegged, carrying their books as though they could take them or leave them. Like they were doing the books a favor by letting them rest against their thighs. *Just walk*, I'd tell myself. But then my books would get knocked out of my arms. "Faggot!"

I'd pretend it was what I had *intended* to do. "Oh good. Thank you, actually, I was literally about to lay my biology textbook in the mud. So you saved me the trouble!"

How did these kids know? Like police helicopters with their giant follow spotlights, they were precocious in their ability to sniff out a homo and at such a young age.

Jonah has that same familiar bowlegged swagger, the confidence and the mischievous grin. *Just walk,* I want to tell myself each time he comes bounding toward me down the hall. But luckily, he's still small enough for me to just scoop him up, kiss his neck, and deflate my junior high school nightmares.

Don and I went back and forth about wanting a boy or a girl. We knew what it was like to have a girl. So fun, familiar, and safe. A boy was scary. Unknown. All that energy . . . and of course, the sports? Don hoped if we had a boy, he'd be just like him: a kid who'd happily stay indoors, reading Jane Austen or darning socks while composing fan mail to Julie Andrews in his head.

But so much of what makes kids who they are—whether they're good at sports, art, music, or math; whether their eyes are crossed or knees knocked; allergic to peanuts or hate tomatoes; even whether they'll wind up dreaming of tight pecs or bulbous breasts—rests securely inside them, predetermined. I'm blown away by how little control they—and I—have over those enormous indicators of how they'll navigate in the world and how the world will react to them.

"It's a boy." Don and I looked at each other.

"Are you positive?"

"Ninety-five percent sure," the ultrasound technician said. "Otherwise it's a girl with an oversized labia."

I bristled. Maybe he was kidding. But he wasn't smiling. I took it in. *Oversized? Really? Eww.*

"Um, how oversized?" I asked the doctor. "And what exactly would that involve? Is there special paneled underwear?"

It didn't matter to Don. He clung to that five percent chance and told everyone, "We're having a girl!"

But I knew it was a boy and I was getting excited about how the new little guy would complete our family. Now we'd have one of each. I was going to be the father of a son. Just like my father was to me. Or maybe not. It suddenly occurred to me that at some point in his life this boy could discover that he might be, you know, *not* gay. Obviously it's a possibility. Just not one I'd ever entertained. Not because I had any prejudice or predisposition against straight guys. I didn't. And I don't. I just don't think about, you know, *them* that often. Because for me, *them* was who I avoided while walking in school hallways. *Them* wanted me dead in wrestling class. And that's how it's always been: there was me . . . and there was *them*. I don't mean any offense. They're the ones who set up the system. And some of my best friends are straight guys. A few are gay, actually, but don't tell their wives.

It's who this country was built by. And for. George Washington. Abraham Lincoln. Scratch that. Maybe not Lincoln. I'm talking about the "men among men." The policy makers. Politicians who twit-pic their balls and hire hookers and score blowjobs in the Oval Office. Men who cheat on their wives and then apologize publicly before doing it again. How about those guys on Wall Street who fucked with our money? Bernie Madoff? Straight. Or the ones who start wars. Donald Rumsfeld? Straight. Osama bin Laden? He doesn't promise virgins for nothing. What about those guys with big fat pinky rings, or those heavily inked motorcycle guys with iguanas as pets? Or those sweaty pear-shaped drunk guys who can't dance, and the ones who wear braided leather belts with pleated shorts, or guys who say shit like "That's what I'm talking about!" Man, I hate that. Guys who call each other "bro" and "boss" and "big guy." Gay guys don't like being called "big guy." Unless, you know, we are. Big.

The year I put tap shoes on the top of my birthday list, I got a basketball hoop. Which wasn't even on the list. I know it never crossed my dad's macho Argentinean mind when I was born that the little baby smiling up at him would one day turn out to be gay. So why was it occurring to me now that our son may very well turn out to be—straight? And why does it even matter? Well, because whether I cared to admit it or not, the whole thing just got a tiny bit scarier. Maybe because it made me question if I could do it. Not hold him and rock him and change his diapers and feed him. Of course I could. But would I be able to truly love him? Unconditionally. Having grown up as a boy tortured by other little boys, straight boys, how would I rise to the occasion of being a man who had to raise one and love him no matter what? How would it feel for, say, a Jew to love a Nazi baby? . . . Too far?

What is "unconditional love" anyway? Does it mean you don't question the love? Because our little devils have a way of trying the limits of our love every single day. The whining alone, which has clearly survived the evolutionary test of time, is a superior test of us parents to see if we're really up to the task. For me? Whining's almost enough to shut down the whole operation. And then there's the intimate relationship we're forced to have with every possible bodily function. We're expected to love despite the vomit. The pee. The middle-of-the-night bed stripping after Jonah had blown mud through his diaper like spin art onto every one of the forty-seven stuffed animals on his bed. And you know what? I'd look at that tiny, stunned face clearly wondering *How the fuck did all that come out of me?* staring up at me, as if to make sure nothing had changed on my end.

I'd smile back at him. "We're good, you and me. We're solid. You didn't shit me away." He'd nuzzle his head on my shoulder. Heaven. It wasn't me versus *them* anymore. It was just *us.*

Our four-year-old, hazel-eyed, towheaded baby is now a happy, curious, loving, mischievous, and really big boy. And like I said before, he already walks with a swagger. As if to say, "Don't fuck with me, faggot, I'll take you out." And there's no question he'll be able to with just a look. But he won't, I don't think. Because even at four he's already the sweetest, most thoughtful and affectionate of giants. That said, I try to stay on his good side. Win him over. But it's not easy. Shit. No matter how hard I try to get him to think I'm cool, he can smell the needy. Jonah is going to see me for who I am. And I him. He's tough. He's fearless. He's a tank. And the worst street fight I had when I was a kid was when I hit Eddie Wade with my clarinet case. May as well have been a knitting bag. Or a tackle box filled with stage makeup (I had one in tenth grade, a prized possession, especially the compartments for medium olive, sallow, and clown white).

I look in his eyes and he in mine. "You're my favorite little boy," I tell him.

"And you're my favorite grown-up," he started saying recently. What could be better? But I can't help but wonder, or is it fear: what if one day he looks at me the way *they* looked at me? I worry that he'll see me, aware of the difference between us, and there will form a divide. Something that keeps him at arm's length. Something that makes him wish I were different. He'll always love me. I know that. But a look like that, from him? I don't know. It would kill me. Then again. Couldn't the very fact that I'm his daddy and Don his papi teach him that love has no divides? I can only hope.

We turn on the music and Jonah immediately perks up. He starts to shake his groove thang, side to side, banging his feet. Arms in the air. The kid can dance. Don and I look at each other . . . a glimmer of hope in our eyes. *Maybe*. Nah. Probably not. And you think about the radical, right-wing halfwits who think the gays recruit young boys into the church of fabulous—as if. Jesus. They are who they are. It's like what we say when the kids reach into the prize trunk at the dentist's office: "You get what you get and you don't get upset."

Jonah struts across the room, crawls across the table, spins around to find this motorized car he got for his last birthday. He lifts it over his head like he's going to throw it. *Just walk*, I think to myself. But he doesn't throw it. He hits a switch and a canned male voice booms from within the toy: "That's what I'm talkin' about!" No. We got what we got, and a gay boy, he's not.

chapter nine

One Fish, Two Fish, Red Fish . . . Three-Way

I have these dear friends, I'll call them Tim and Ron. They're among the few gay couples without kids who didn't drop us the second they saw our daddy diaper bags. They're actually an old boyfriend of mine and his partner of fifteen years who live in Northern California. And they have a life very different from ours. They spend most of their free time in the great outdoors—weekends hiking with their dog, traveling to spas and gyms and parks and nude beaches. And it's at these beaches where they occasionally meet others who like to join them for meals, hikes, or—or a shower. Together. After which, they fuck. These guys engage in the occasional *three-way* or two. Not all the time, they assure me, but on vacation or whatever, they'll meet a guy and, in a scenario that seems completely implausible to me, the guy comes home with them and they all have sex. You believe that?

How on earth does something like that happen? I have trouble imagining it:

Hi, I'm Dan, this is Don. Did you have any trouble finding the house? How do you like that hybrid? Pinot grigio? Which of us would you like to blow first? No. It's preposterous. Who are these guys? They're not twenty-two. They're like me, you know, over thirty. And for some reason, I can't seem to stop thinking about it. Maybe because my life is so markedly different.

I recall the promise I made to myself when we decided to have kids, that not everything in our lives would change. I particularly didn't want to become one of those parents whose house transforms into a receptacle for plastic toys, bubble wands, big-wheel tricycles, and giant, colorful play kitchens that eat up huge corners of space. I didn't want to be one of those parents who stopped going out, seeing friends, and having one-on-one time with their spouses beyond the marathons of bad reality TV after the kids have fallen asleep. I didn't want to become that guy who no longer had regular sex with his spouse because he was so damn tired and so instead lived vicariously through the stories told to him by friends without kids.

I think you can guess what happened.

So. Among other things, we do wind up hearing a great deal about our friends' libidinous appetites. I don't think we solicit it. Perhaps there's a look in our eyes that screams out, *Please tell us it hasn't ended for everyone!* Or perhaps they insist on telling us every detail of their sex-capades because, well, they're jealous. That's right. They are green with envy over the blessings children have brought to our lives. Oh, who am I kidding? I'd kill to be like them.

I do notice they tell only *me* about their adventures. They don't tell Don. What's that about? Are they trying to pick me up? That's so fucked up. And very flattering. How dare they!

I hope they never stop. How lucky they can be so open. It's bound to end in disaster. Why can't I be more like *them*?

As if I could ever. Who am I kidding? I never had a three-way even when I was single. And then after I met Don, forget it! Not his cup of tea. I brought it up to him once, over a cup of tea, actually, and he said, "No way. I'll just wind up being the guy holding the towels."

I wish I could blame my kids. For all of it. If it weren't for them, the sky would be the limit, right? Three-ways. Fourgies. Whatever! But as I said, I wasn't that guy *before* kids, so what makes me think I could be that adventurous now? What bugs me is that now I don't even have the option. I can't ever become the kind of guy who has three-ways. It's over for us. That's right. Forget holding the towel, Don, we've *thrown in* the towel on anything remotely fun in that nude beachy kind of way, at least until the kids are twenty. And by then I'll be a hundred. And fat–*ter*. And unable to find *one* person who'd want to touch me, let alone two.

And I can't blame it only on my partner. Although it is pretty much his fault. If I have to be completely honest? My God. I am just too damn tired. Forget a three-way. I'm too exhausted, usually, for a two-way. Or frankly a one-way. Too tired. And the simple truth? *I'm just not that into me.*

Even though I want to be the kind of person who still has a lot of sex, I can't even imagine how to make that happen given the amount of energy it takes to get into some semi-willing state. Then the energy to remove articles of clothing–buttons, zippers, snaps, watches, socks, oh God–and then to convince my partner in some seemingly spontaneous but completely strategized plan of attack that a little sex might be a nice idea. And why? 'Cause it's really that fun? Not really. After a day of kids, I'm a little over the charm of moist human discharges.

We spend most of our one-on-one time telling each other the latest cute thing one of the kids said in the tub. Or analyzing the cut, clarity, and color of our son's poop while referring to each other as "Daddy" and "Papi" even when the kids aren't around. Sex isn't real high on the to-do list for the time being. We'll settle for being Mr. and Mr. Vicarious, who soak in every last detail of our friends' *sex-tracurricular* activities when we have the chance to see them. Like this past Christmas. Only this time, the topic somehow shifted to another hobby we heard about.

"Wait a minute. You—what? You *shave* your *balls*? Um . . . why?"

"I like it," Tim says. "I like the way it feels. So does Ron."

Stop. I don't want to hear anymore. Sorry I asked. But wait: was this the one thing I'd neglected to do in the endless list of things I've tried to keep the spice in my marriage?

New cologne. Check.

New workout equipment. Check.

New haircut. Check.

New story of how some guy flirted with me at Starbucks to make Don jealous. But Don doesn't get jealous. Check.

Shave balls? No way. What purpose does it serve? And how do you become that guy? Who the fuck is that guy? And is smooth-balled guy the same as three-way guy? 'Cause I wouldn't mind being him, but if I have to shave my balls? Nope, I'm out.

Don and I drive home in silence. Then I break it: "That was fun." I'm looking out the window.

"Yeah," he says, "those guys are great."

"Yeah. Love them. Love how they're so . . ." Long beat. I look at Don. Then a longer beat. Then: "Have you ever—?"

"No," Don answers, cutting me off. Another long beat. I can't let it go.

"Would you ever—?"

"No." And that's that. Case closed.

We're just not those guys. And that's okay. I look over at Don, and feel so relieved we have each other. And after all these years that we've been able to trust each other long enough to build a family together. *I'm happy.* Isn't that what's important? I don't want anyone else in our bed unless it's just our kids, who crawl in after a bad dream or for a little morning cozy time.

We get home and I get ready for bed. Brush. Floss. Mouth guard. Eczema cream. Mmm, sexy. Hand cream. Heel balm. Trim the eyebrow hair that looks like it's trying to get jiggy with the one sprouting out of my ear. Be older, Dan. Anti-aging face cream. Anti-aging neck cream. Eye serum for fine lines and puffiness. Then I see the razor sitting on the counter by the sink.

It calls to me: *Come on, Dan, I dare you. Do it, Dan. Do it. What're you, afraid?*

I lock the door, grab the razor, and drop my shorts. Here we go. First few seconds, no problem. Wow. That *is* smooth. I *am* that guy. I'm that guy!

I take my eye off the ball(s) for one second to smile proudly at myself in the mirror and *ouch!* Fuck! The blade goes over a bump. There's so much blood! I wrap with tissue and pull my shorts up. I did *not* just do that . . . I'm not standing in my own bathroom with one shaved ball and a lot of blood and–*shit!* Not only am I not that guy, now I'm the guy who tried to be some *other* guy by shaving his balls instead of owning the fact he's not that guy and being okay with the guy he is.

I'll pretend it never happened, I think. *It'll grow back.* I put all thoughts of "that guy" out of my head and run out of the bathroom. Don looks up at me.

"You were in there a long time. You feeling okay?"

"Oh, yeah. No. I wasn't sitting on the–I mean, yeah, I'm fine. I was clipping my–I had my razor and I dropped my–I'm thinking maybe we should get a small fridge in the bathroom–for cold water and maybe some ice. You know?"

He looks at me, oddly *not* surprised that I sound like a crazy man.

"I'm going in to do story time with the kids," I say, putting an end to the whole thing.

I get to the kids' room and sit between them on the tiny love seat. Each puts their head on a shoulder. Best moment of the day. Certainly of *this* day. I open my favorite book and start to read: "One fish, two fish, red fish, blue fish . . ."

Maybe it was the loss of blood, but my mind raced to another of the boys' stories about some hunky guy at the train station who came home with them.

"Read it, Daddy!" The kids can tell I'm distracted. I try to focus.

"One fish, two fish, red fish, blue fish. Big fish, small fish, old fish, three-way . . ." Yep. They met this guy at the station. And apparently they almost had sex on the train.

"Daddy! Read!"

I pick up a different book. "I do not like green eggs and ham. I would not eat them in the rain. I would not eat them on a train." On a train, huh? "I do not like them, Sam I am." I'm not Sam. Who is Sam? Is he cute? Do you think he'd want to have a three-way?

"Daddy!"

I have to stop. I can't keep thinking about this. I look at my kids' beautiful faces. What's wrong with me? *Why on earth would I want anything more than what I have right now?*

I do not want to be that guy who has a three-way, I can't lie. I do not want him in my house. I do not want him with my spouse. I'm happy with the guy I've got and playing Daddy, wiping snot. I do not like green eggs and ham. I've learned to like the man I am. I am not short, I am not tall . . . I'm just the guy with one smooth ball.

chapter ten

I'm Not as Competitive as You Are

"Do you love Jonah, Daddy?" Eliza so innocently asked from the back of the car.

"Why do you ask, honey? Do you think I'm mad at him?"

"No, silly Daddy!" She laughed. "But do you super much love Jonah?" she further investigated. I wondered if I should correct her grammar. It was way too cute. Like when she says "It very hurts." I'll hate it when she stops. But that's what videotape is for, and she does have to get into college.

I smiled as I figured out what this love prodding was all about. Obviously a sly little plan to curry favor with her daddy so she could feel a tiny bit more special than her brother, entitling her, perhaps, to a bigger helping of dessert or an extra sheet of Trader Joe's dried seaweed snack. (Don't ask me why the kids love these. I'm just so grateful they're made of actual seaweed and not some corn-syrupy gummy snack that'll turn her tongue green.)

"Of course I love Jonah, sweetie," I said, "he's my boy. And you're my girl. I love you both—"

"Just the same," she finished my sentence with the preschool equivalent of an eye roll. She'd heard this many times before, just as I'd heard it hundreds of times from my parents when my sister and I used to ask whom *they* loved more. I smiled.

"Yes, honey, just the same. And more than you can ever imagine."

And then, as she gazed out the window through her Tinkerbell kaleidoscope—the remains of a goodie bag she found under her booster seat—she said, "Even though Jonah doesn't want you?"

I almost drove into a mailbox. "What, sweetie?" I was unsuccessfully trying to keep the panic out of my voice. She repeated it. I processed the words slowly in my head. What on earth was she thinking? Of course I had to consider the source, yet I suddenly got a sinking feeling I remembered from my first job waiting tables in New York at the Manhattan Chili Company. After a week of watching me drop ponderous bowls of chili on the floor as I tried to balance ramekins of chopped onions on the knuckle of my thumb, the staff prepped me for my inevitable firing. Had Jonah been slipping hints to his sister that "things weren't working out"; I may not be cut out for this kind of work; and he was going to have to consider "making a change"?

Fuck that. I'm the daddy, I told myself, my grown-up maturity, self-confidence, and authority at war with a ridiculous yet deep-seated need for my kids' approval.

"What do you mean, he doesn't 'want' me?" I asked, through my very best trying-to-act-casual laughter. Eliza explained.

"Jonah only wants Papi to put him to bed. Not you. Papi. Only Papi."

Now I could see where this was coming from. And it was true, around this time Jonah was going through a particularly intense bonding thing with Don. It was amazing, actually, how Jonah would call Don his "buddy" and he'd look for him first in any room. It was heartwarming and sweet. I loved seeing how bonded he was to his papi. Did I have the occasional pang of jealousy? Sure. But I knew kids go through phases. Sometimes Papi is the favorite. "Sometimes" as in "sometimes the sun comes up in the morning." And *sometimes* Jonah asks for Daddy. "Sometimes" as in "sometimes there is an earthquake in your backyard."

"Eliza, that's okay. Sometimes you want Papi and sometimes you want Daddy. And the same goes for Jonah. We all love each other. It's okay." And of course what I said to her was true. But if I had to be honest, there are times it doesn't exactly feel like a warm bath of love when the kids would only seem to want Don to do bedtime, read stories, sit next to them, you name it.

"Papi, can I drive in your car?" Jonah whines.

"Me too!" Eliza pipes in.

"No, Jonah, today you're driving with Daddy!" Explosion of tears.

Or in the morning: "Papi, sit next to me!" Eliza calls out.

"No, Eliza. Papi sits next to me!" Jonah argues.

"I asked first!" Eliza's voice gets louder.

"*No!* You got to last time!" Jonah now shouts.

Don squeezes between them on the bench. "Look, guys! You can both sit next to Papi." The kids smile from ear to ear. So does he, and I'm not sure he's trying to hide it.

Hooray! Yippee! Papi saved us from having to sit next to

mean, stinky, boring Daddy, who played with us all morning before making pancakes and then balloon animals and who looks like he's tired and possibly a few pounds heavier than he was yesterday! I'm not actually so shallow as to think the kids don't love me. Of course they do. One kid inevitably wants one parent over another. And I love Don. And he loves me. But I still can't help that feeling from childhood, deep within me, of not wanting to be picked last or to be blamed for things I didn't do.

A while back we took the kids out for pizza. They split a small pie but it was a lot. We packed up Jonah's extra piece to take home. On our way out of the restaurant we saw a homeless man sitting against a parking sign. Don took the bag with the extra slice and gave it to the man. Jonah had mixed feelings about it, to say the least. But Don turned it into a teaching moment. Last week we happened to be passing the pizza place and Jonah, out of the blue, asked me why I gave his pizza away.

"I didn't, pal. Remember? Papi gave it to the homeless man," I explained.

"No! *You* gave it away, Daddy!" He started to cry.

"Oh, Jonah. I get that you want that pizza now. But it was a nice thing for Papi to do. Papi gave that pizza to the homeless man. Not me. Papi." I tried to stay cool.

Don laughed. "What can I say? I can do no wrong in his eyes," he gloated. "It's called diplomatic immunity!" But I wasn't about to take the rap for someone else's crime.

"It was Papi, sweetie. *Papi* gave it away."

"No, Daddy. It was *you. You* gave my pizza to the man!"

"It was not!" I sounded like I too was only four years old.

I laughed uncomfortably. Don found it hilarious. Sure. Because he was the one getting away with murder! How did he do it? I tried not to hate my husband for this innate ability to curry favor.

Lately Don's been offering the kids his iPod Touch to watch movies or TV or to play a game while they're in his car. I don't let the kids watch TV in the car because I think they watch enough television, frankly, and I enjoy my time in the car conversing with them, playing music, singing songs, or just listening to them talk to each other. Is my way better? Natch. I get full points for that one. If I could only get them into my car!

Dan: "Don. Tell them they can't watch in your car so that they don't throw a fit when I say I'm driving."
Don: "I'm not doing that. I don't have the same fear of them watching iPods in the car."
Dan: "Um, it's not a fear, actually. It's called 'guidance.' A healthier choice. But you offer any kid on the planet a car made of cookies, gumdrops, iPods, and baby bunnies, and they'll want that car!"
Don: "So what does that tell you?"
Dan: "Just because they like it more doesn't mean it's better for them!"
Don: "And just because they hate it, doesn't make it the healthier choice."
Dan: "Hate. Wow. Okay. *Fine!* You win!"
Don: "Feels better to say it out loud, doesn't it?"

Are we more competitive with each other because we're both men? I don't know. I only have my own experience by which to gauge. I know Don grew up willing to throw almost anyone under the bus, even the bus driver, if it ensured him an A+, front seat, top tier, gold star. And where was I? Just as competitive, fighting to rescue that bus driver under the tire, so maybe I'd get singled out as a hero—possibly with a piece about me on the eleven o'clock news.

But I don't think I was born this way. It was something I learned. As a kid. The way kids pick up things from parents who want them so desperately to feel like winners because the parents so clearly don't. Like Jonah, I too have an older sister. But here's the thing: I don't recall feeling competitive with her as a kid. I mean, we both clearly waged an unconscious war for the attentions of our parents. But it never felt like my goal was to beat her. I was the baby, a full three and a half years younger, so I was able to squeeze some extra points out of that. I was always singing for my supper, putting on shows, acting like a clown, and generally trying to overcompensate for the fragile, anxious, bed-wetting gay boy in training (GBIT) that I was. I managed to get a lot of attention from my parents, thanks to both the anxiety and the clowning. Did my sister resent me for it? Probably. So I overcompensated. I supported her when she was struggling and I tried to lift her spirits when she was down.

One of my earliest GBIT memories is of her winning the Barbie beauty pageant held by her friends in our building in Manhattan. Even at four I remember feeling a pure joy and relief I've rarely felt, if ever, since. I was similarly invested in my sister's winning a spot on the junior varsity cheerleading squad. I almost cried when she made the squad. Perhaps, sadly, maybe even happier than she was about it.

"Smile more this time!" I'd coach. "Louder! Say it like you *mean* it! And the left leg is starting to lag on the eagle jumps. You're going to want to watch that." She'd jump and cheer, then look at me for feedback.

"Good! Do it again!" I'd shout. She'd jump and cheer.

"That's it! Yes! You're awesome," I'd cheer back at her. I remember feeling happy. Like it was us against the world and we would be okay as long as we stuck together. Perhaps seeing nearly everyone else as an obstacle to my happiness wasn't the healthiest of attitudes, but it did foster a drive to work together with a partner against a common enemy.

So why now all these years later does this competitive drive of mine surprise me so much in my relationship with another man, living, working, raising a family? It doesn't always feel like we're working together against a common enemy. It's trickier, navigating the power in our marriage and our roles as parents. Who decides what? Who compromises? I think there are certain unwritten rules in the straight-parent couples I know. Dad's voice is heard but Mom's is listened to. She dictates the schedule, the menu, and the itinerary. The who/what/where and when. And Dad doesn't even try. But in a same-sex couple? It can sometimes feel like two magnets approaching each other from the wrong sides. Here's a conversation Don and I have had, sadly, more than once:

Dan: "I told the kids they had to be in bed by seven thirty."

Don: "Oh, I told them they could watch a movie."

Dan: "Right. But I said no movie. I don't want to back down and lose all credibility with them."

Don: "Right. But wouldn't I lose credibility if I back off the movie thing?"

Dan: "Or you could come off as supporting what Daddy said. What movie?"

Don: "*Over the Hedge*, and how about *you* coming off like you support *Papi*?"

Dan: "That movie is rated PG."

Don: "So? It's animated. It's cute. It's not scary."

Dan: "Maybe it's not scary to you, but to a three-year-old? You know what cortisol is? It's a fear hormone secreted in the brain. Movies like that trigger—"

Don: "Okay. You're fucking crazy, you know that? What gets secreted in their brain from having a fucking crazy daddy?"

Dan: "I'm crazy for caring about what my kids are exposed to? According to commonsensemedia.org, that movie's not for kids under ten. Our kids are five and three. That doesn't even *add up* to ten!"

Don: "I guess I just don't care enough about my kids to pick a movie that freakyself-righteousparents.com recommends. You're a better parent all the way around. Congratulations. You win!"

Dan: "Feels better to say it out loud, doesn't it?"

All the issues a man has in this society about feeling relevant and powerful, productive and successful, multiplied by two? It's tricky, being a man in a relationship with another man who is also by nature competitive. Add to that the fact that we're two creative artists straining to catch a drop or two from the stingy tit of show business in a place where any of us would gladly shove even our closest friend into a box of fast-metabolizing jelly donuts if they came even close to standing in our light. We who were damaged by our invisibility as children are dragging our loved ones into this giant stew of need and guilt and money and shame and ambition with nothing but a Barneys Warehouse Sale to make us feel better. Then we have kids. And the focus becomes them. And we strive to push our competitive impulses aside to work together to make a great life for them.

In a relationship between two men the balance of parenting power can be trickier when both are strong, smart, opinionated people who like to feel in control and *right* most of the time. On the other hand, Don surrenders on a lot of the stuff he just doesn't like to do or doesn't care about. Which is healthy. He lets me be the one to get woken up at six for that cuddle after a nightmare or to change wet pj's, the one to take out a splinter, buy clothes, feed them (though he toasts a mean Pop-Tart), dress them (in clothes that fit), or make vanilla French toast in the shape of woodland creatures. This adds to the sting when both of them would crawl over live snakes and broken glass to be the one who gets to sit next to Papi at a restaurant or in a movie.

But then something happened. I overheard some friends of ours—a straight, married couple with two small kids—in the middle of a giant fight during one of our park picnics together.

Him: "What are you doing?"
Her: "I'm giving them a snack. It's a fruit twist."
Him: "You realize they just had lunch about twenty minutes ago. And B) that stuff is pure crap."

Her: "I bought it at Whole Foods!"

Him: "So what? You think a 'fruit twist' grows in nature like that? It doesn't. It's processed. And check the grams of sugar. What is it? Forty? Fifty? Like a can of Coke. You're throwing me under the bus."

Her: "Okay, wow, cranky. Are you insane? I'm not—"

Him: "Yeah, you are. You give them the message that what Daddy says doesn't matter but what Mommy says is law."

Her: "Someone needs to grow a little self-esteem, there, buddy."

Him: "Someone had plenty before someone's *wife* hacked away at it."

Her: "Along with his balls, apparently."

Ouch. Silence. The conversation stopped there when they realized several people had overheard them. So much for my whole theory about navigating the power between parents in a same-sex relationship. I have to admit, it was a relief to find out that there's nothing particularly gay or straight about anyone's ability to compromise or delegate or work as a team in a marriage with kids. It's just about our own egos and our own willingness to relinquish control. That's right. Watching another couple struggle in the same way really inspired me to let some of this shit go.

The truth is? I like seeing the kids with Don; their bond with him is so strong and affectionate and specific. And it's different from the one I have with them. Which is a good thing. They get different things from the both of us. There's balance in that. And what's more, I love doing all the things I've come to do for the kids. And with them.

Don and I both notice how we go in and out of being Flavor of the Week. It's not a reflection on our worth as parents. On how much they may love one of us or the other. Or on our weight. Although last summer we were swimming and I had forgotten to wear the surfing rash guard shirt—what we affectionately call "modesty shirt"—which I use to cover the parts of me for which push-ups and Pilates seem to be no contest. Jonah took one look at my naked torso and burst into tears, screaming, "Black shirt! Black shirt!" as though my exposed upper body would leave him with a visual he couldn't boil away if he tried. Believe me, I know because *I've* tried. Hmm. Maybe if I could get Don to drive shirtless, the kids would pick my car . . .

chapter eleven

More Than I Can Chew

It's the Sunday before Memorial Day. Don's home while Jonah naps, thank God, so I'm taking Eliza to buy groceries at Trader Joe's. She loves Trader Joe's because the guys there always give her a balloon. Eliza has an odd little obsession with balloons. She sees one and has to have it. But then, as if it were a seven-layer wedding cake or a nuclear warhead, everyone has to get out of her way when she's holding it. She walks slowly. Staring at it. And if it accidentally rubs against anything and makes that awful squeaky sound, she screams as if bloody worms were about to ooze from its nozzle and pull her hair. And yet she worships it. And hates herself for having to have one but loves it all the same. Basically, it's me with a York Peppermint Pattie.

We're in a hurry and I know I can't devote that kind of attention to a pink floating nuclear warhead, so I lay down the law—"No balloons this time"—as we tear through the store grabbing everything we need for our barbecue tomorrow. Turkey burgers, hot dogs, chips, salsa, and drinks . . . I load all the bags in the car, strap Eliza into her booster, and race down Ventura Boulevard.

Then I see Pier 1 and remember I'm supposed to get a

patio umbrella. I pull into the parking lot. The only open spot is in the blazing hot sun. I think, *Oh good. I can preheat the hamburger meat.* I prep Eliza for a fast errand.

"Okay, monkey, we're just going in and getting the umbrella and going right home. You can help pick the color. But super fast, okay? Because we have meat in the car and don't want it to go bad."

"It's not bad. I love meatie!" she says. And she does love meat. Maybe it's her midwestern bloodline or some other primal carnivorous craving buried deep within. Eliza holds the string of the balloon I said she was forbidden to have. She stares at it as if eye contact alone will keep it from popping.

"That's right. Meat is good as long as it doesn't spoil. You understand, honey? If the burgers sit in the car too long, they can start cooking." She laughs at this. Then I tell her we have to leave the balloon in the car. She doesn't want to let it go. I have no time to negotiate. "If you bring it, it will pop." She's not buying it. "It will pop. And it will be very loud. And then it will die and everyone will cry." Done. It's not exactly a lie. It *could* pop. Whatever.

Inside, we head right to the patio umbrellas. They come in green, orange, and beige. Oh, and a striped one. I know we definitely *don't* want that one but can build a case in favor of any of the others. I hate how indecisive I am. Having seen and admired the R. J. Cutler documentary *September Issue*, I'd vowed to be more like Anna Wintour in my everyday life. *Which color umbrella, Dan?* says my inner Wintour. *Don't be a pussy. Pick the right one or you're fired. Simple as that. There can only be one* right *choice.*

Eliza reminds me that green is my favorite color. Yes. Green is good. But in a decidedly *un*-Anna Wintour move, I take out my BlackBerry and snap photos of the color choices and email them to Don. Meanwhile, a very cute twenty-something salesclerk approaches wearing this cool lime-colored polo shirt. He tells me he's a big fan of my work. "You were Billy on *The Comeback*!" I don't get recognized all that often so immediately I have the fantasy of asking him to come over and say it all again—*and this time, say it slower!*

"I really loved *The Comeback*," he says—a phrase, like the old "friend of Dorothy," which has come to mean "Yes. I am, indeed, gay." I love him. And not just because he loves me. He heads to the basement to find a nine-foot green umbrella since the floor samples are too small.

"Your daughter's adorable," he says over his shoulder. I smile, thinking, *So are you.* But I don't say it, of course. I'm not *that* guy, either. Then I look around. Where is my "adorable" daughter? Just before going to the panic place, I see her emptying a basket of colorful animal-shaped soaps onto the floor in aisle five. I run over.

"Bet those animals are pretty clean, huh?"

"Smell, Daddy!" She holds one up to my nose.

"Mmm . . ." I almost gag. It's cherry or berry or, wait, yes—it smells like a urinal puck. I want to sneeze. I think about the hamburger meat in the back of my car. Shit! I have to hurry.

"No, sweetie, we're not buying soaps today," I say.

"Just one, D-D? Just for today?" she asks, her eyes begging. *D-D* is what she calls me when she wants something.

CuteGaySalesGuy comes back just in time for me to demonstrate how sweet yet firm I can be. I feel myself unconsciously suck in my stomach. "Eliza, you were smart to pick the cute soaps, but we can't buy—"

"I have to go potty, Daddy!" she cuts me off, jumping up to her feet.

CuteGaySalesGuy leans the various umbrellas against the counter. Eliza retreats behind my leg. "How'd you go about becoming a dad?" he asks.

I love that he's asked. What a great opportunity to tell him about the process, to encourage him, to be a role model. I want to give him a conscientious answer, but Eliza has to pee and my car is transforming into an In-N-Out Burger.

"We adopted. But listen. Don't go anywhere," I tell him, "we're going potty." I don't want him to think I'm blowing him off.

Eliza and I step into the men's room. I hate public restrooms. Just because men can pee standing up doesn't mean we should pee hopping on one foot. How else to explain the urine on *every single* surface? Eliza and I have a rule we chant over and over as we step into bathrooms: "Don't touch anything. Don't touch anything." And we don't.

To prep her bum for perching, I wrap the seat in layers of toilet paper like some intricate Egyptian mummification process. I listen for a tinkle. I don't hear anything.

"Go pee-pee, monkey . . . we have to hurry." I feel guilty for rushing her but will feel even worse if two hundred bucks' worth of food is ruined and CuteGaySalesGuy doesn't get to adopt. Finally I hear a short tinkle. Now we're talking. Eliza wipes, pulls up her pants, and flushes. We wash our hands. I'm rushing as always but I make up little songs as I rush, hoping not to stress her out.

"Get our fingers in the water and then rub, rub, rub. Then the soap, do it quickly and then rub, rub, rub. Rinse and grab a paper towel. Grab it. Now. *Now. Now!*" She sees right through my game.

"I'm going as fast as I can, Daddy," she says. Which, frankly, is a much sweeter way of saying, *Cool your jets, bitch, you're stressing me out. And incidentally, Papi is waiting for us at home so you may want to tone down the flirting.* Which I would deserve.

"Stop singing," she says. I smile. She's right. I count to ten in my head.

"Let's go, Eliza," I plead.

"I'm coming, Daddy, I'm coming." I run up to the cashier's desk as I hear the chime of my BlackBerry. Don likes the striped umbrella. What? I apologize to CuteGaySalesGuy for his trouble and get him to sell me the floor model of the striped one.

"I don't need the box. I have groceries in the car and it's hot and . . ." Eliza rolls her eyes. When did she start doing that? She's five! And have I really mentioned the groceries that many times?

CuteGaySalesGuy pulls down the floor model. He seems eager to chat. "How long did it take you guys to adopt?"

I want to tell him my story. I want to be encouraging. I have a responsibility, don't I, to the gay dads of the future?

"Come on, Daddy, let's go!" Eliza is whining. Perfect. It's like my value as a father, my identity as a gay man, my ability to pay it forward, and my skills as a barbecue host are all being tested. And I'm failing at all of them. But come on. Right now my single responsibility, besides watching my daughter, is to *get that fucking meat home!* Why did I have to buy the umbrella and grocery shop and take Eliza all at the same time? Why did I agree to host a stupid barbecue? Why did I agree to do all the prep and planning? Why did I agree to have kids? I've definitely bitten off more than I can chew. But I'm sure Anna Wintour could handle it. As I'm digging for my credit card, I try to give CuteGaySalesGuy some helpful information.

"It took eighteen months," I say, "from the time we met with a lawyer to the time we took Eliza home. Best thing that ever happened to me—to us." I hate how cliché and preachy I'm starting to sound. I go on, "But that's just me. I'm not one of those people who think you don't know what love is till you have a kid. Of course you do! I mean, I loved a lot of people before having kids—and things. Pad Thai, for example. Love it. Always have." I remember that the last time the kids heard me speak of my love of pad Thai, Eliza asked me if I wanted to marry it. The answer, of course, is yes. But I think the gay plate is kind of full, so to speak, on the marriage equality fight already. Plus I think filing joint taxes with a bowl of rice noodles and fish sauce could get tricky.

He laughs a little, then stares at me blankly, not knowing how to take what I'm saying. I don't blame him. I just likened my kids to an Asian entrée. I'm self-conscious. "I just mean, parenthood . . . it's fantastic but not for everyone. Is there a dolly I could wheel this out with?"

Eliza tugs at my pants, whispering, "Daddy, I have to go poopie." *What?* She did *not* just say what I think she said! We were just in the bathroom and there was no mention of a poopie. I don't have time for poopie. Poopie was not in the picture.

"Eliza, I'm paying and then we can go poopie at home, okay?"

"No! I have to go right now!" She starts to cry. CuteGaySalesGuy notices. I'm a better daddy than this. I hand him my credit card.

"Why don't you run my card. I'll be right back," I say, forcing a smile though there's clearly panic in my voice and fury in my eyes. He smiles empathetically. I fall in love with him just a little more. I have a quarter-second fantasy about my life with CuteGaySalesGuy—driving around in a Range Rover, our child who never has to go poopie in the car seat and a whole aisle of Pier 1 loot we scored with his employee discount in the trunk. Oh, and he's not wearing a shirt. And I look like Ricky Martin. What? It's my fantasy. Or was. Eliza's still crying.

"I know," he says, "you have meat in the car." He smiles. Winks, maybe? Or I imagined that. I'm mortified. I run to the bathroom with Eliza.

"Don't-touch-anything-don't-touch-anything!" I chant, faster than usual. I gift wrap the toilet seat again and Eliza sits. But nothing happens. She shrugs.

"Don't look at me, Daddy. I don't want you to see my poopie face." I didn't realize my daughter *had* a "poopie face," but I do as I'm told, facing the wall. I position myself so I can glance in the mirror at her adorable mozzarella face as she squeezes out a turd. She really is the cutest thing I've ever seen. How did I get so lucky? So blessed. So—shit! The meat. I turn to face Eliza.

"Is that it, sweetie?" Nope. I turn again. She starts chatting now that she's comfortable. And relaxed. Why shouldn't she be? So adorable and infuriating. I try to appeal to her, calmly and rationally.

"Eliza? Remember all the food we bought together? All those yummy hamburgers and hot dogs we're going to make? Yeah. Well, Daddy's got to get that food home so we don't have to throw it all in the trash. Okay? So will you do Daddy a big, super big favor and go potty right now so we can get home before it's too late?" A part of me is hoping a little added stress may jolt the crap right out of her. Literally. But come on! She did *beg* to go to the bathroom only *three minutes* ago.

What's the use? By now there's probably a hungry, ketchup-carrying crowd lining up behind my car, and I've undermined the future of the gay movement by failing to deliver more than a few cursory words when I should have been inspirational. And here I am, facing a pee-stained wall at the Pier 1 Imports' men's room—all for a tacky striped umbrella I've decided to buy because I am *nothing* like Anna Wintour.

Finally she's done and we flee to the checkout. CuteGay-SalesGuy has given me thirty percent off! I'm speechless. "Floor model discount," he says, smiling at me. Oh my God. Should I ask him out? Oh no, right. I have a kid. And another one at home. And I'm *married*! Hellooo? I sign the receipt, thank him profusely, and wish him luck.

"Definitely check out Vista Del Mar adoption services," I say, dragging Eliza and my new umbrella toward the car.

I hope I've done my duty to future gay dads. Because I definitely have *not* done my duty as a dad, to be patient and loving and understanding of my five-year-old, who didn't ask to be dragged around on errands with me, even if I did cave on the balloon thing. The only one who's done her duty today—in both senses of the word—is Eliza. And good for her for taking care of herself. Because after all the stress and anxiety I put myself through, the meat was fine. And CuteGaySalesGuy? I can't be responsible for him and his parenting choices. Right? What do I look like? Let him Google "gay adoption" if he needs more hand-holding. Not my problem. And he shouldn't wear lime. Not that shade of lime, anyway. What is this, Miami?

Oooh. That feels good. Very out of character for me. And *very* Anna Wintour.

chapter twelve

Room 207

We're all squeezed into a row toward the back on a flight back from DC. We have been visiting my sister and her family. I've already taken half a Xanax and the kids are busy coloring in activity books. As the plane revs its engines and speeds down the runway, I offer to take Eliza's hand.

"I'm not nervous, Daddy," she proclaims.

"I am," I admit to my six-year-old. She looks at me to see if I'm serious.

"You're supposed to be the grown-up," she says. Busted. I'm relieved Don didn't hear her, as he'd undoubtedly flash me a raised, kids-say-the-darndest-things eyebrow and a smug little smile.

The flight is fairly smooth, no turbulence to speak of either outside the plane or in. As usual, Eliza and Jonah are very well behaved on the trip. They love to fly. They color and play games and watch movies on our iPods. No tantrums. No running down the aisle. No kicking the seat in front of them, like the monster toddler currently kicking mine.

Don is sitting across the aisle from me, as he usually does, reading voraciously and listening to music. He and I will switch seats midflight "if necessary." But it never comes to that. When we land, the kids unfasten their seat belts and stand, patiently waiting for their turn to deplane. Several other passengers shower us with compliments about how well behaved they are and what great parents we are. "What a couple of angels," someone says as they pass our row. Sure. Now they seem like angels. After six hours in a confined space with limited snacks, piped-in oxygen, and dizzying flatulence coming at them from every angle. But put them in a hotel? That's a different story.

There is something about the place we book on our trips to visit my sister that always stirs up trouble. I don't know what it is. Nor do I know why we always stay in the same hotel and in the exact same room. Three times now we've gone and all three times we've stayed in room 207 at a chain hotel that adds "Suites" to their name so that it sounds fancy. It just means there's a microwave and a sink in the room.

Our first experience with room 207 was when Jonah was two and Eliza was four. We got stranded at the hotel for almost a week after a blizzard hit the area. And not just any blizzard. An epic, worst-storm-since-1937 kind of blizzard. Two feet of snow piled up and left us stranded while the city of Gaithersburg, Maryland, caught up with the task of plowing the roads. The kids were in heaven. They got their first experience with snowmen and snow angels and snowball fights. Keeping them entertained wasn't ever an issue. But on the afternoon of the second day we were going a little stir-crazy and the hanging of wet, snow-drenched clothes along the radiator in our room was getting a little old. My mother, visiting at the same time, had taken the room right above ours. The kids got used to bopping upstairs to visit Abuela and back down again.

At one point, I had gone outside to scrape ice and snow off our rental car with a broom and a dustpan like a true West Coaster and Don was tidying up the room. I sent the kids upstairs to visit with Abuela. I was outside for maybe ten minutes when I heard the noise. The fire alarm was sounding loudly and persistently from inside the hotel building. Oh my God. I dropped my broom and ran toward the building. Once inside, I noticed all the guests coming out into the hallways to see what was going on. *Clang, clang, clang, clang* . . . the alarm kept going, echoing loudly. Eliza had Jonah by the hand and was walking down the stairs when I entered the building. They met me in front of the door to our room. Eliza had a look of panic in her eyes and she was yelling, "Jonah pulled the button! Jonah pulled the button!"

Jonah had gotten out of Abuela's room and run down the hall like any normal, curious, fearless, "terribly two" little boy and reached up to pull down that deliciously tempting and just-within-reach fire alarm handle that must have been calling to him since we'd arrived. For a split second I was even impressed with the restraint he'd shown up until then.

"Jonah!" I got down on my knees in front of him. "Show Daddy what you did!" He walked me to the end of the hallway and pointed to the small alarm box he had activated. I think the relentless ringing of the alarm paired with the look of panic in the guests scrambling in the hallways was enough to ensure he'd never do it again, but I hammered the lesson home.

"You may never, ever, *ever* touch a fire alarm. Do you understand?" I wanted to add to my fire alarm warning something extra that would really sink in, like, *If you touch it, your head will explode and worms and blood will fly out and make you die.* That felt extreme, not to mention highly inaccurate, but I was desperate to differentiate this particular scolding from the dozen or so I'd given him over the past few days. "Please don't pull all the towels into the tub with you"; "Don't climb on the curtains"; "Don't stand on the table"; "Don't play hide-and-seek unless someone has agreed to 'seek' *before* you hide under the housekeeping cart, throwing Papi and Daddy into a full panic that they've lost you forever." Right now Jonah was staring up at me as he always does during a reprimand. He wanted me to pick him up. He cried with pure heartfelt remorse. He wrapped his arms tightly around my neck. "It was a askident," he kept repeating again and again. My heart, yet again, was broken.

I called the front desk to get someone to shut off the alarm. The seventeen-year-old "manager" informed me that only someone from the fire department could reset the alarm.

"Okay. So when can they get here?" I begged.

"Yeah. Don't know. Roads pretty hairy. Haven't been plowed. Still coming down. May not have chains on the trucks." That was his response. Little morsels of bad news, delivered with apathy and distraction, packaged in odd little "Me Tarzan, you Jane"—grunty caveman sentences with nary an article or pronoun. I thought I would lose my mind.

"But the alarms are going off, loudly. Nobody can stay

in their rooms with all that noise. Isn't there anyone who knows the building well enough to reset the alarms?"

"Yeah. No." That was the end of that conversation.

What if there had been a real fire? Would the fire department have been unable to come and rescue us? What a terrible system! I guess nobody knew there would be a blizzard. And I guess we all knew, now, that there was no *real* emergency. No harm had been done besides our feeling of total humiliation. It was mortifying to have to look at dozens of guests standing in the hallways, some still in their pajamas. Don thought we should explain how we had lost control of our two-year-old son and as a result ruined all of their vacations. I wondered if we couldn't just act like one of them—baffled by the alarms, annoyed even, as we'd say, "What the hell happened?"—as though we had no idea who or what had pulled the trigger. But it was too late. Don was already going person to person with an explanation and an apology. Don, who always seems like he's running for mayor of every fucking hotel floor, airport security line, or fast-food dining area ("Anyone need straws? I've got enough for everyone!"), had blown our cover. It was during this episode that I went through my regular checklist of regrets. Why did we have to come to DC in the dead of winter? What's so special about my sister's family anyway? Why did I agree to meet Don at that stupid Celebrity party in '92? Why couldn't we have stayed at a nicer hotel? Why did we have to have kids?

We waited a full hour before the fire representatives walked through the corridors to determine that, in fact, there was no fire and it had been, as we'd said repeatedly, an "askident" caused by Jonah. Right around this time, Frank, the father of the seventeen-year-old manager, arrived. He was the Director of Operations for the hotel. My mother decided this would be a good time to lodge a complaint.

"This cannot be!" she said indignantly, her accent stronger than it should be after fifty years in this country. "A hotel needs to be able to shut off an alarm if it goes off accidentally!"

Frank was apologetic but explained that the fire department mandated all alarm activations be investigated. My mother wasn't having it.

"But we knew there was no fire. You can't just have them blaring for an hour while people wait. Come on! That's no way to treat hotel guests!"

I couldn't quite believe her chutzpah to try and blame the hotel for my kid's hijinks. But I was relieved to have the attention shifted off us. We quietly filed back into our rooms and prayed the memory of the last ninety minutes would fade quickly.

My mother got an elaborate fruit basket and her room comped. I think the guy also asked her out. I was impressed. Clearly at these "suites," the customer *is* always right. Even when the customer's grandson is most definitely wrong. Oh, and when we got back to Los Angeles, I got an effusive email from Frank, apologizing for our discomfort and offering us a free night the next time we were in town and wanted to stay. As if!

A few months later, we were going east again. This time for Passover. With that free-night coupon burning a hole in my mailbox, I booked room 207. I thought the kids would be more comfortable if they recognized the room. Jonah was just barely a half-year older and a half-year more mature. He said repeatedly that he would not touch the fire alarm. I couldn't help wondering what kind of havoc he *would* be willing to wreak.

The first night, we put the kids to bed in the bedroom and Don and I decided to sleep on the pullout couch of the adjoining living room. We were on West Coast time, so the kids were wide awake until about midnight. Suddenly, just as I was finishing up the last bedtime story, I noticed Eliza was scratching her head. A lot. I switched on the light for a closer look. Yep. Crawling in and out of strands of her platinum blond locks, a sly, disgusting, cocky little louse. Immediately, instinctively, I started scratching my own head. That's when she started screaming: "Lice! Lice!" We'd just recently gone through this at home and she'd picked up from us that lice were the devil. I shushed her as though it would make it less true. I pulled both kids out of the bed and started stripping the sheets. I calmed her down a bit as I frantically looked through Jonah's hair to see if the little bug had siblings. Thankfully, Jonah's scalp was clean. Oh, no, there was one. Damn it. Don threw on his coat and shoes.

"Where are you going?" I asked, desperate not to be left alone with the little critters who were now infested with little critters. It was all too much.

"I'm going to find an all-night pharmacy."

"What for? All they'll have is Rid," I warned him.

"So? I'll get that!" He was already halfway out the door.

"It's pure poison," I told him.

"Great. Then it won't take long to kill them."

"You mean kill the kids." I knew I was being a bitch. But what did I really want? One of us had to go and get something to put in their hair. And I didn't want to drive out into the night almost as much as I didn't want to stay alone in that hideously cursed room 207.

"No!" Don protested. "I'm not even going to get into this with you right now. I'm sorry they don't have lavender oil or coconut juice or the yolk of a dove's egg or whatever the fuck you think will kill them naturally. But it's one in the morning and we're desperate!" And he was gone.

Eliza started screaming again. She felt something crawling down her back. She was convinced that eggs were hatching in her scalp and millions of bugs trying to bite her. This, of course, only made Jonah scream. So that was fun. At around 1:30 a.m., someone knocked at my door and asked that we "keep it down." I glared at the guy. I mean, honestly. It wasn't like we were having a kegger and blaring a dance mix all night. Believe me. If I could have "kept it down," I would have. I wanted to tell *him* to "keep it down," but well, that would have been ridiculous and hysterical and irrational, all things I was feeling. The poor guy wasn't wrong. My kids had, in fact, woken him up and I felt terrible.

I threw both kids into the bathtub. Amazingly effective at calming them down, I must say. Don got home with the battery acid for the kids' hair at 2:30 and by 3:00 both kids were asleep. I know lice have become a problem for families across the country—across all regional, ethnic, religious, and socioeconomic landscapes. But there's just something about it that makes you feel marred. You have cooties. And nothing short of boiling your bedsheets, toys, clothes, and okay, even the kids themselves will truly rid you of them. You're tainted. Forever. At least that's how it feels.

On our third and final stay in room 207, one of the kids wet the bed in the middle of the night—which hadn't happened in over a year and felt completely arbitrary. We chalked it up to the travel stress. Oh, and the bedtime milk boxes for which the kids had campaigned by jumping on the beds singing "Just this once" over and over again. Sorry, ever since my sister's cheerleading days, I'm a sucker for any kind of synchronized chanting.

We called the front desk to get a new set of sheets. The housekeeper arrived, a middle-aged woman who had clearly never been introduced to Spanx and didn't seem to care. She was the very definition of jolly. She entered the room and insisted on changing the beds for us. Delighted by the kids, she asked them tons of questions and told them all about her own. She looked at their bed and then over to us and our pullout couch. She tried to take in the whole scenario as she headed out of the room. Then she turned back.

"Is that the little boy who set off the fire alarm last year?" she asked. I was completely shocked the story had made Suites lore. Had nothing else really happened at this place in a whole year to erase that silly incident from people's minds? I guess stories of lost room keys and jammed soda machines couldn't compete.

"Yep. That was our Jonah. I suppose everyone heard about it." This makes her laugh. More than she should.

"Oh yeah," she says. Then she looks around again and finally asks boldly, "Um, where is their mother?"

It's not like I haven't gotten that question before. It happens, from time to time. Usually in places outside the bigger cities, which serves to remind those of us lucky enough to get cocky about how "normal" we feel in our lives as same-sex parents that it's not like that everywhere. It's good to be reminded that, oh yeah, this is weird for some people. So I usually have understanding and patience when I answer the questions from those who just don't have firsthand experience with us gays. But something about her assumption sets me off.

I have been known to respond like a total asshole. I'll either pretend not to speak English or I'll start looking around, as though I only just realized that their "mother" is missing. But usually, I take a breath, ignore the insensitivity, chalk it up to ignorance, and explain our family. On this day, I found the question particularly offensive because of the context. She was making a correlation between the fire alarm incident with Jonah and the absence of a traditional mother in our family.

Where is your chin? I wanted to ask her. *There are just so many of them, it's hard to suss out just the one.* I wanted to hurt her. No. I wanted her to know she had hurt me with her question.

"Well, I don't know where you're from, but this is America. And even if we don't have the same rights you do to marry the person you've committed your life to, we do have the right to start a family. So maybe you're too closed-minded or coldhearted or just plain ignorant to be able to imagine that two men could be parents. But guess what? We were fortunate enough to be part of an adoption plan with a wonderfully generous young woman in Wisconsin, not just once, but twice . . . blessing us with the opportunity to give our kids a loving home and a well-rounded education, which is clearly something you missed!"

She was stunned. "Um . . . no," she said. "I just remember you all from last time. There was a woman here. Short, curly hair?"

"Oh. That was my sister," I said, turning red and hoping that this, in fact, would be the moment of my death.

As she headed out the door, she turned back quietly. "I apologize. I guess I was mistaking her for the kids' mother." Weirdly, she didn't stay for the rest of the Q&A.

That would be the last time we would stay at that particular hotel. Clearly not for any fault of the place or its staff. There was just something about room 207 that brought out the worst in us. I also avoid that room number at every other hotel where I stay now. Just to be safe.

chapter thirteen

Sexy Look

I took the kids to a Winter Wonderland holiday party last year that very well may have spoiled any other party the kids would ever attend in the future. It was almost hostile in its fantasticness. It surpassed my wildest imagination of what a kids' party could deliver. These people went all out. They re-created the North Pole with real snow, reindeer and sleigh rides, a snowman bouncy, crafts, a candy cane bar, photos with Santa, you name it.

At one point the kids were delighting over two out-of-work actors dressed as Mary Poppins and Bert, performing magic and songs. They, meaning I, loved it. Especially the part where they turned a white hankie into a bowl of Tootsie Pops. A spoonful of sugar really does help—well, you know, help you forget they're not *really* who they're dressed to be. That was until one of the bright-smiled performers, Mary, who like everyone else in L.A. would do anything to "make it," possibly even porn, walked around passing out postcards for her industry showcase called "Desperately Seeking—Representation."

I too performed for dozens of children's birthday parties when I was in high school, delighting kids with balloon animals and kiddie illusions as The Great Houdanni. So I felt a bit overprotective of my performing comrades. I clapped and whistled a little louder, perhaps, than I should have.

"Did you see that?" I shouted at Eliza and Jonah. "That hat was empty a second ago! Right? Where'd those Tootsie Pops come from?" I was genuinely impressed. "These guys are amazing, aren't they?"

Suddenly, one of the moms turned to me, annoyed. "Tootsie Pops? Really? Why am I the only one who cares what goes into my child's body?" She went on and on about how every single lick on a lollipop delivers corn syrup and refined sugar and artificial colors into the bloodstreams of our children, creating a chain reaction that compromises their health. Every single time!

Okay, Stressy Tessy, calm down! I thought to myself. I mean, who wants to be the parent who begrudges their kid a sucker at a birthday party? Especially one given to them by Mary Fucking Poppins? So what if, after the party, she turns into adult film star *Cherry* Poppins? I didn't want to be that dad.

I now look at my watch and realize we are into hour two. The kids are being shuttled from the Mary Poppins station to the Cotton Candy pavilion. They're all squealing with delight as they line up to receive pink sticky clouds of refined sugar and artificial color.

I should pull Eliza and Jonah from the line, I think. *It's too much sugar. I'm compromising their health and they've already had lollipops, snow cones, and who knows what else. Can't these people throw a party with carrot sticks and organic cheese squares?* Stressy Tessy had obviously gotten into my head.

I intercept the cotton candy lady. "Eliza and Jonah are

going to share one!" The kids start whining. Other parents groan.

"Oh, come on," a burly dad says to me, "it's a birthday party! What's wrong with you?"

"Just pacing ourselves," I explain. "I know cupcakes are in their futures. Just teaching them a little something called moderation and *compromise.*"

The parents snicker. I overhear a cacophony of responses: "Poor kids . . . It's a birthday party! They've got *him* as a parent—isn't that compromise enough?" Ouch. Where's Stressy Tessy to back me up here?

I know the key is knowing *when* to compromise. How bad is a cupcake once in a while? Have you ever *had* a red velvet cupcake with cream cheese frosting? My God. It has to be a hell of a lot better than, say, the emotional damage from depriving yourself of one. It's a worthwhile compromise.

The following week Don took Jonah to a superhero party and I was supposed to take Eliza to an all-girls "glamour party" for one of her classmates. I didn't really know what a "glamour party" was, but it sounded right up my alley.

The party was held at a high-end beauty salon that had been taken over for the birthday. At first, I have to admit, I was dazzled by the unlimited access to this buffet of fabulousness: the brushes, combs, curling irons, makeup palettes, rows and rows of nail polish! And stylists and manicurists on hand to give makeovers. I heard a familiar voice behind me say, "Welcome! Enjoy a vegan snack!" I turn to face the voice and it's Stressy Tessy! "Oh, hi!" she says, lighting up when she sees me. "Hello again!" I say, then explaining my surprise that she's the birthday girl's mother: "I didn't put two and two together."

"Yep! That was crazy last week, huh? But my snacks? All organic and gluten-free. And the juice boxes are coconut water. So you've got nothing to worry about! Your kids are safe. At least for the next two hours." She laughs a lot at her own joke. "Help yourself to a glass of champagne while the girls get ready for the red carpet!" It's only eleven a.m. but I can tell she's not on her first glass. I thank her as Eliza runs to an empty chair to begin her beauty treatment. Then my auditory processing kicks in. "Red carpet"? I am not proud of the thirty minutes that followed, as it way too slowly dawned on me that my daughter was getting hair and makeup in order to be photographed by a team called "Party-razzi." While Eliza enjoyed the hair, nail polish, and makeup treatment, she looked like a deer in headlights on the red carpet in a sequined dress with a feather boa, hearing her name being shouted out: "Eliza! Eliza! Right here!" She looked only at me the entire time, as if to say, *Daddy? What the fuck am I doing here? You* are *still my daddy, aren't you? DO SOMETHING!*

Stressy Tessy was standing behind the line of "pho*kid*raphers" shouting for all the girls to line up with hands on their hips. "Okay now, ladies, give us your sexy look! Right here! Sexy sexy sexy! Right here!"

That was it. I'd heard enough. I reached onto the carpet, grabbed Eliza by the hand, and made a beeline toward the exit, scurrying past trays of spelt cookies, carrot sticks, and fruit-juice-sweetened zucchini muffins. We only stopped once to grab our party favor—a bedazzled faux-leather handbag ostensibly to hold their faux car keys, faux BlackBerry, and faux Virginia Slims.

"Where are we going, Daddy?" Eliza asked me. "We left before the cake."

"I know, babe, but you know what? It was time to go. And I'm not sure you were having so much fun with all those photographers taking your picture. Right?"

"They were loud."

Asked and answered. What on earth was Stressy Tessy thinking? Kids grow up fast enough, don't they? Without having to formulate a "sexy look" by the age of five. I let her ruin the last party for me—and ultimately for my kids, after I dug through their party bags to discard all the candy. But you know what? I'd risk rotting my kid's teeth every day of the week rather than rotting her soul with gobs of lip gloss and a child-sized bustier at a Playboy bunny–themed birthday party!

"Are you disappointed, sweetie?" I'm feeling guilty about the way we stormed out of there.

"I wanted to stay for the cake," she says, simply.

"Honey, that cake was made of birdseed and mulch. You wouldn't have liked it."

We get to my car and I strap her into her seat. "You know what we're going to do? We're going to get ourselves the biggest, most delicious, gooiest candy-covered cupcake we've ever seen. One that's got sugar cream on the inside and is dipped in chocolate and covered with candy and then dusted with sugar! And after that if we want, we're going to get another one! How does that sound?" Eliza's eyes light up.

Eat your heart out, Stressy Tessy with your "sexy look." We'll see you in the dentist chair.

chapter fourteen

Faster, Pussycat, Swim, Swim

"Go, Dazzlers!" I scream at the top of my lungs the second I hear the referee blow his whistle. I'm at my daughter's Saturday AYSO game. I notice some moms sitting on a blanket behind the goalposts, talking about a new brand of fruit leather that is made from organic pear puree. I have a *lot* to say on the topic but feel a gravitational pull toward the dads standing on the sidelines discussing strategy and encouraging our five-year-old daughters in hot pink cleats to be aggressive, pass to their teammates, and drive the ball toward the goal. I notice Eliza is standing in the field picking a Cinderella tattoo off her arm as the ball rolls in her direction. I have somehow become a combo platter of soccer mom (minus the minivan and L.L. Bean jeans) and closet soccer dad. "Eliza, look!" I shout. "The ball's all yours! Give it a kick, honey! Pretend it's the head of Ursula from *Little Mermaid*! *Kick it!*"

She looks up, half-interested, hops up and down like she has to pee, and watches as one of her opponents intercepts the ball and takes it in the other direction. She looks at me, smiles, and shrugs as if to say, *The ball does what it wants . . . isn't that weird!* It's adorable. Kind of. I smile and give her a thumbs-up, covering my frustration. I'm not going to be one of those dads who scream on the sidelines of their kids' games. I'm not.

I walk back over to a cluster of dads who are midconversation.

"I think we need to schedule an extra practice during the week. Teach these girls some basic passing skills." I hear this suggestion lobbed into the air. Who said that? Wait. Did that come out of me? All the dads are looking at me and nodding. I *did* say it. What the—? Who *am* I?

I'll tell you who I am: I'm the guy who put Jonah in a cute little tennis clinic with an amazingly patient and sun-damaged pro named Ray. Five three-year-olds face the net. Ray tells them all how to hold the racket and they comply. He tosses each of them the ball and they swing and try to hit it. Most miss. Jonah lands it perfectly in Ray's court, just before the baseline. And then he does it again. And again. Ray turns to me and smiles. "Say hello to your retirement plan." My chest fills with pride. I want to cry. It's like he said it about *me*. This is *not* a good sign. To get that invested in the performance of my three- and five-year-olds?

Oh shit, it hits me, *a second ago I was Joe Dad, suggesting extra practices for the girls. And now I'm a vagina away from being one of those frantic "real-sized" moms running dance drills and spray-tanning their kids for the pageant circuit.* What the hell difference does it make, really, how well they play at this age? Or at *any* age? I mean, of course it's nice to find something your kids are good at. But this feels different. More personal. Sadly, more like redemption.

I was never good at competitive sports. Never. And I

tried. And my dad really tried. To get me to be good. Or better. Or just not embarrassing. The chubby, five-foot-three Argentinean with a Napoleon complex was obsessed with proving to the world he had a lot of power despite his stature. Which explained the basketball hoop I received on my eighth birthday instead of those tap shoes I'd put so prominently at the top of my wish list. And the at-home pitchback net, which I used only once, as a pretend *I Dream of Jeannie* bottle where I served tea to my sister's Barbie and Ken. The equipment was all part of my father's campaign for more athletics.

We lived in New York City before moving to the suburbs. What did I know from kickball, baseball, and soccer? I was a city kid. I liked going to Phil's Pizza after school to share a slice and a grape Italian icy with my best friend Amy. Then we'd go learn double Dutch from the neighborhood girls, whose dads were dealing crack in the playground behind our building.

Fast-forward to a year later and we're living in the burbs with a yard and a mower and a neighbor who calls me "Jew bag" and a basketball hoop in our driveway. Suddenly I'm trying to "break in" my catcher's mitt with some high school jock my dad hired to coach me. No surprise there, given my dad's obsession with the whole idea of coaching. He loved that word. *Coach.* For a while there, he wanted me to call him Coach. It was creepy, 'cause he so wasn't one, not to those gifted with sight and hearing. But he tried. He even became my team's soccer coach one year as part of our town's recreational sports program. He showed up to the first practice with handouts, flip charts, and some Argentinean fight song.

It just gave the assholes *another* reason to kick the shit out of me on the bus.

"Hey, Danny Fuck-a-ten-speed!" they'd shout at me.

I'd close my eyes and imagine my retort: *Oh. I get it.* Hah! Hah! *Because "Bucatinsky" and "Fuck-a-ten-speed" rhyme! Or wait, what? They don't rhyme? Oh no! Your careers as greasy-haired preppy rappers are over, assholes. Not to mention the fact that a person can't actually fuck a ten-speed. Do you understand that? Maybe not. You'll probably be the guys who die trying.* But instead I said nothing. I pretended not to hear them. Yeah. I wasn't so much into the bullying.

But these guys were relentless: "Tell your dad he's a loser coach and we're gonna lose. Okay, faggot? Is your dad a faggot too? Maybe the apple doesn't fall far from the faggot." Boy, did they double over laughing at that one.

Needless to say, soccer didn't work out so well that year. But I didn't let that stop me. Nope. Over the years, I played them all: soccer, basketball, baseball, and tennis, each worse than the one before. Though I was never forced to do any of them, I remember feeling like a disappointment if I didn't. To myself. To my parents. My tireless effort to try different team sports was my way of mitigating that disappointment.

But I hated sports. Almost every single aspect. Except maybe the uniforms. I did love those. Hello! Why the hell did it take me until I was twenty-five to come out of the closet? If anyone had paid attention to the boy in his baseball uniform, dancing in the mirror on the door of that closet, they could have saved me a lot of trouble. I remember the baseball team in fourth grade. Our uniform, modeled after the Yankees', was almost worth the hassle of playing on the team. I wore it with pride until game time and then I felt nothing but dread. One fateful Saturday, however, I limply held up my mitt more to block the sun from my eyes than to catch a fly ball headed right toward my face. I remember feeling the blinding sun, pretending it was a spotlight, and wondering, *Is this what Doug Henning feels every night, center stage on Broadway in* The Magic Show? Suddenly the ball careened into my glove, managing to break my finger in two places before rolling onto the ground. I was benched–in uniform, thankfully–with my middle finger bandaged and splinted into a semipermanent "fuck you" for the rest of the season. It was heaven! But I don't think my dad was too happy about it. After all, he'd invested all this money in a pitchback and balls and gloves and the coach who got seven bucks an hour to run drills with me. Luckily for me, my athletics career didn't end with soccer and baseball.

The summer after sixth grade I joined a local swim team. I never thought of swimming as a competitive sport. But I'd promised my parents I'd sign up so I wouldn't have to go to some sleepaway camp that featured a midsummer Olympics. Are there scarier words for a gay kid to hear than "midsummer Olympics"? Camp seemed, at the time, like a fate worse than death. Little did I know that swim team would be a fate worse than, well, sleepaway camp.

I was pretty nervous that crisp May morning of our first hometown swim meet. I dove into the water. Some combo of the cold and my own panic left me breathless. Literally. I gasped and sputtered. But I wasn't drowning. I wasn't. It must've looked like I was, though, because suddenly everyone started screaming, the pool was cleared, and our swim coach, in a gesture of heroism, hit the surface of the pool in his polo shirt and chinos. Everyone was staring. When I reached the edge of the pool, my mom was there to help pull me up. I burst into tears. The sheer humiliation was more than I could handle. But everyone applauded with relief. "Thank goodness you were rescued!" Not a sentiment I shared at that particular moment. Now I had to live with the infamy of being "the loser who drowned in the shallow end" for the rest of junior high and high school. Ridiculed for it. Tortured by it. I should have gone to camp! I think I would have gone, had my parents found one that didn't focus on sports. Couldn't they have sent me to dance camp? Cooking camp? Or roller-skating-in-the-garage-pretending-to-be-on the-*Donny-&-Marie*-show camp? I would've rocked any of those.

I finally got my first whiff of victory in eighth grade in a dance competition at Nancy Finkelman's bat mitzvah. I was hooked. Turned out I liked the smell of victory as much as the next guy. I just preferred the scent of the hustle or the hora over a line drive straight to third. But more than the feeling of the win, I'd discovered something far more valuable and important in my development. I had found something I was good at that I also loved to do. I'd found an activity that made me feel good. Shouldn't that have been the point all along?

• • •

The Dazzlers are now tied with the Magic Mermaids. There are only five more minutes left of play. Don is reading some

Victorian novel on a giant blanket behind one of the goals. Jonah is chasing after a ball with another kid. It's a beautiful day. I ask myself if I'm having a good time. And yes, I am. Again, isn't that the point? I tell myself it doesn't matter if the Dazzlers win. I tell myself it doesn't matter if Eliza dribbles or runs fast or kicks the ball, passes it or ignores it altogether. We're here as a family on this Sunday to connect with other families and one another—and to have fun. Eliza runs up to me on the sidelines.

"Daddy, can I have a sip of water?" I notice Eliza has managed to scrape off all but Cinderella's head from her arm. I reach into my bag and hand her the pink "Eliza" thermos. She drinks.

"Are you having fun, Eliza?" I ask. She nods. But I want to be sure. I get on my knees. "Seriously, sweetie, you don't have to play if you don't want to."

"I want to." She smiles, handing me back the thermos of water.

"Good, Eliza. I'm glad," I say. And then I can't help myself: "Have fun. Do your best. And don't be afraid to pass that ball. Or kick it and drive it toward the goal!"

"Okay, Daddy!" she says. And we both know she's going to do exactly what she wants to do. "Did you know that after the last game we all get trophies?" Her eyes are like giant blue twinkling planets. She turns and skips happily back onto the field to join her teammates.

And then, as though she's planned it, as though she's colluding with God or the universe or Destiny or whatever, the ball rolls to Eliza and she dribbles it down the quarter field she has left before reaching her opponents' goal. She kicks it hard and it dances into the goal! I jump up and down and scream!

"Yay! Good job, Eliza! Woo-hoo!" Eliza high-fives her coach and the other Dazzlers. And the game is over. They've won. Eliza scored the winning goal. The other dads come running over to hug it out and high-five Eliza. She turns to me and Don with this heartbreakingly touching smile, both embarrassed by the attention and relishing it, trying not to reveal how proud or happy she really is. Oh my God, she's trying to act "cool." It's the cutest thing I've ever seen. As usual, I start squirting tears—not over my own pride, though. I'm touched by the pride on my own daughter's face. And I'm overjoyed by this feeling of affirmation and belonging that comes from just being a guy with his husband and kids at a soccer game. Sounds so simple, yet it feels like something I only dreamed about growing up. Maybe this is what my dad was after all along.

I hope we all come back next week and do it again. You know, if the kids *want* to. The more she plays, the better she'll get. Nothing wrong with that. I wonder if they make a pitchback net for soccer.

chapter fifteen

A Giant Valentine for a Tiny Heart

I thought parenthood would magically make me more empathetic and give me a more generous soul. And as far as putting my own needs behind those of my children, that has absolutely happened. But once in a while, I want—or dare I say, need—a little reinforcement from my kids. No, I'm not proud of it. I'd love to be a "high road" kind of person. But I'm not. I am at times pretty small. I know I am. And I often find myself looking admiringly at the beautifully paved "high" road from where I'm driving, down here on the bumpy, potholed, gravelly low road.

Case in point: I come home after a particularly discouraging day at work to find the kids painting in their little smocks, swirling vibrant colors against paper clamped to the easel.

"Hey, that's beautiful! Is that the sun?" I'm genuinely impressed.

"Yes. And the ocean. And a volcano. And a rainbow. See?" Eliza is proud of her work. I am too.

"I love it. May I have it?" I imagine it on a wall in my office.

"Nope. It's for Papi," she says, as though I should know better.

"Cool!" I say, forcing enthusiasm. "He's going to love it."

"You can have Jonah's painting," she offers, without looking up.

"No! Mine is for Abuela!" Jonah announces about his purple swirls.

"What a great idea! We'll send it to her as soon as it dries," I say, hiding my disappointment.

There are about two million works of art piled into a giant Tupperware tub in the back of our closet. I can have as many kids' paintings as I want. But today, damn it, I want them to *want* to make the painting for me. "It's the thought that counts." And I'm all about being in their thoughts on this particular day and have somehow deluded myself into thinking that the painting is an accurate indicator of their love and appreciation for their daddy.

A particularly low point for me was a recent Valentine's Day. The kids and I spent hours the night before, cutting out little hearts, gluing red fuzzies, feathers, and stickers on homemade valentines for classmates, babysitters, and teachers. We even made a beautiful painted frame with "I Love You" written all over it for Papi. We knew Don would *love* it. And he did. But the morning of Valentine's Day, I looked around the kids' room, I searched the table, the playroom, even the floor, and nowhere was there even a sign of a valentine for me. I knew it would be best to leave it alone. And a bigger person might.

"Hey, kids! Did you make a valentine for Daddy?" I forced out, half laughing at the absurdity of having to ask (well, of *course* they have a valentine for Daddy) and half sheer humiliation.

"Nope!" they announced proudly.

No? They *didn't*? I started to feel something bubbling deep within me that I can only describe as a battle hymn. That's right. My inner Tiger Mom was only wishing I *had* a card I could throw back in their faces to put a little more thought into. I'm tired of them getting off so easy. God forbid they feel a sense of duty and responsibility and gratitude. Damn it. And worse was forcing me to sound like a hundred-year-old curmudgeon blasting "kids these days." I guess the real question: Why the fuck wouldn't they *want* to make their daddy a Valentine's Day card?

I was dying to ask them why. But that's such a dangerous question. What are they supposed to say? *Because we don't think of you; because we forgot; because we don't like you; because you've put on a few pounds; because when it comes to the list of people we want to make valentines for, you're in the C-loop, and we just didn't get to the C-loop this year.* The truth is, they're little kids. Who gives a shit? What does it matter? I know they love me. I *know* it. So forget about it. Who needs a stupid piece of paper with my name spelled wrong and a scribbly little heart drawn around it? It's not a measure of how much my kids think of me—or love me. It's not. I decided to let it go.

A minute later I was filled with hate. And not just for them. Why didn't any of the other people in their lives encourage them to make their daddy a valentine? I clomped up the stairs to find Don.

"Do you know why the kids didn't make me a valentine?"

Don looks up, almost bored. "I'm sure they did," he says. "I would know, don't you think?"

"Maybe they forgot to give it to you." He knows that's not what happened.

"They didn't forget. They just didn't make me one," I tell him.

"All right. Couldn't matter less. It's creepy for kids to give them to their parents. It's a holiday for couples. And it's not even a real holiday. It's all crap." Lucky for me, he's never been a fan of Valentine's Day.

"Spoken by a man with a giant valentine frame with feathers and tissue and glitter I was up until midnight hot-gluing so the kids could present it to you when they woke up." I try not to sound bitter.

"Well, I loved it." He smiles at me. Like that's supposed to help.

"You're their parent," I say, as it occurs to me. "It's your job to make sure they remember to make me a valentine. It's a sign of respect." I like the way that sounds as it comes out of my mouth—laying down the law. Like something a Tiger Mom might say. Or better yet, Anna Wintour.

"I guess I forgot. Okay. But anyway how's that going to feel? When you know the kids are bringing out a card they made because I told them to?"

"Better than this hot-glue burn feels on the back of my hand."

I walked out of the room, deciding again to let it go.

That afternoon, I was driving Eliza home from her school Valentine's candy-palooza and she was stacking all the gifts and cards on her lap. I looked at her through the rearview. She was so cute putting them all in neat little stacks, deciding which lollipops to eat today and which ones to save. I told myself, *Let it go. Don't say anything. Don't say ANYTHING . . .*

"Eliza?" I asked. *Don't do it!* "It feels nice to get a valentine, doesn't it?" She nodded, her mouth and tongue bright red from the cherry-flavored heart she was sucking on. *Don't. Say. Another. Word.*

"Uh, quick question: why didn't you make a valentine for Daddy?" *You did it, asshole! Couldn't help yourself!*

She looked at me. Very still. Like she was really taking in the question. Like she was about to say, *Oh my God. Daddy. I completely forgot. Will you ever forgive me?*

Instead she gave it as much thought or weight as I should have given it in the first place. "Daddy. I have a great idea! If you let me have *one* more candy now, I will skip dessert after dinner."

And when I saw the whole bag of stupid Disney ads masquerading as valentines in the trash at the end of the night, I realized where my real valentines were. They were fast asleep in their little beds upstairs, open books in their laps, lollipop sticks stuck in their hair, crashed out from all the sugar.

chapter sixteen

Keeping Them Off the Pipe and the Pole

"That's it, huh? If they don't strip or do drugs, you'll be happy?" My friend Cara busted me over chopped salads after I announced that I, like Chris Rock, merely want to "keep my kids off the pipe and the pole!" She could easily see through my bluster that I was way too neurotic to leave so much up to chance.

Cara has five kids. She doesn't even think about parenting as something that needs to be addressed anymore. She feeds them. Gives them clothes. Helps them with their homework. Done. She says they can work the rest out in therapy. I envy her ability to surrender and, when I am with her, try to be just as cool. But it's not me. I know it's hard to believe, but I have a hard time with surrender. I'm constantly looking at my kids and worrying about what kind of life they'll have when they're grown. They are still too young for us to get any real sense of who they may become as adults. Right now they love to spin till they're dizzy, jump naked on the beds, and sing "Shake my bootie, shake my bootie." One might say they're a tequila shot away from dollar lap dances.

When Don and I first debated whether to adopt or use a surrogate, I remember discussing how many kids were being born each day that needed families. Foreign adoption was closed to us, so we chose open adoption. People often referred to it as heroic. But there are always more parents wanting to adopt newborns than there are newborns to adopt. There was nothing heroic about it. We wanted to become parents. Not to save anyone. Also, and less obvious maybe, was our discomfort with the idea of surrogacy. We wanted to avoid any awkwardness about a child who would be biologically linked to one of us and not the other. ("Look at little Andrew, he's got cankles and throws like a girl! That's got *you* written all over it!")

But most appealing, I think, was this idea that we would be so filled with gratitude at having been able to have a family that we wouldn't put as much pressure on ourselves or our children. We thought that after such a difficult and unconventional process, the gratitude would keep us from getting sucked into the rat race and the pressure to excel.

But in time, I've realized that it's not enough. I've listened to other parents and watched enough soul-killing reality shows to know how much of it is out of our hands. What if we've done everything right? We love them and support them and get them a good education. And they're socialized and confident and well-adjusted. And then they're teenagers and have a bad day and look for comfort inside a crack pipe?

All the control I like to imagine I have is just bullshit I do to make up for the fact I actually have so little. The nature-versus-nurture debate bubbles up again and again. Especially when you've gone the route of adoption.

Once my kids were in preschool, I became painfully aware of the *nature* part of the equation. Kids come hardwired with their own drives, interests, strengths, weaknesses, talents, shortcomings, and propensity or aptitude for learning. No matter what I do, I can't reconfigure the DNA that makes them who they are. Which isn't to say I don't believe in the power of the environment in that whole nature/nurture tug-of-war. But so much of what colors the *way* we nurture may also have a genetic component as well.

Eliza and Jonah are surrounded by smart, dynamic, mature kids who've been reading since age two. I overheard one dad in the schoolyard the other day bragging about how his son's Mandarin teacher took him to eat dim sum, "and little Matthew ordered in Chinese! You believe that?" No. I don't. Another four-year-old in Jonah's preschool class is already playing the violin. I want to tell everyone to fuck off and let these kids be kids. But that's just what all the parents say whose preschoolers *aren't* playing instruments while conjugating verbs in Latin. We've been reassured by their teachers that kids learn at different rates and that eventually it all evens out. It's not easy to see, yet, what kind of learners my kids are going to be. Especially since, like their two dads, they *hate* feeling like they're being evaluated.

I never learn, though. I'll be holding up a Montessori board with the letter *A* on it. "What letter is this, Jonah?" He laughs and says, "Poo poo." That's appropriate, he is just being a four-year-old boy. *Appropriate*, incidentally, begins with the letter *A*. How hard is that? *When should he know his alphabet?* I wonder. *Or does he already know it and want me to bugger off?*

"Jonah, seriously, what letter is this?" Jonah looks at it, processes it, and decides: *"T!"* He moves on to a giant yoga ball and pounds it with a wiffle bat. I'm pretty sure he's imagining the yoga ball is my face. Tell me he doesn't notice the frantic, sweaty look in my eyes that probably makes him want to slam shut and pack it in.

I try to remain calm as I turn my attention to Eliza's schoolwork. It's a short reading comprehension exercise. Only two sentences. And then I have to ask her three simple questions. Oh, how I hope she remembers what I'm about to read. I'll do it cleverly. I'll make it a game.

"Oh, this'll be fun," I say to her, but already she sees right through it. "I'm going to tell you some fun little secrets about a girl named Mary and then I'll pretend I don't remember and you can remind me!" I start to read.

"'Mary went to the store on Monday. She needed to buy a bag of apples.' Got it?" I ask her, smiling.

Eliza looks at me. She so doesn't feel like playing this "game" with her daddy. But it's homework, so she'd better get used to it.

"Shoot. I forgot who went to the store." I look to her for the answer.

After a beat, Eliza responds, "Bag." I look to see if she's kidding. Please be kidding.

"Can I use your iPad?" she asks.

"Not yet, sweetie, let's just do this one fun activity. Ready? Listen carefully: *Mary* bought *apples* at the store. So, what did Mary buy?"

I should just accept that she's not into it. Take my cues from my child. That's the right way to handle this. But how will she get into college if she doesn't know where Mary went? Everyone knows that *Mary* went *to the store*. I just said it a second ago. She's buying apples. Mary fucking loves apples. It's all she ever buys.

"It's apples, sweetie, remember? And who is buying the apples?" Eliza can't remember. Can't? Or won't. Maybe this is all just a plan to mess with me and make me crazy. If it is, it's worked. I give up and hand her the iPad.

I wish I could be more like Cara and just leave them alone, but have you ever watched the show *Intervention* on A&E? It used to be our favorite show in that fishbowl kind of way. We were on the outside, looking in. That was until we had kids. But now? I'm in the fishbowl, people. The show does nothing but torment me. All I do is think how all those drug addicts out there have parents. Sure, some of the parents were abusive boozers and drug addicts themselves. I'm not talking about them. I'm talking about the other ones. The ones who may as well be me. The ones who always did their best, put their kids first, had the noblest of intentions, and then found a crack pipe in the bottom of their kids' backpacks.

Every episode of *Intervention* begins with some twenty-two-year-old smoking crack or meth, shooting up, or inhaling Dust-Off spray. Then we hear about how they sell their bodies for drugs and only come home to their parents when they've run out of food or clothes or money for drugs and need a place to crash after a four-night drug binge with homeless crackheads with whom they've been having sex and to whom they are quite possibly engaged to marry.

"That won't happen to us, right, Don?" I ask. Don's been sober for thirty years and should have insight into an addict's mentality and triggers that can be avoided by those who have the "disease" of addiction. Instead, Don spouts a particularly old-fashioned point of view:

"Oh no, our kids are being raised in a good family. They're not from a broken home." Is he kidding. He usually then turns on the parents, blaming them for their bad haircuts and trashy outfits. "That mom does not have the arms for sleeveless! No wonder her kid's sniffing glue! Oh. And the dad's a homo." Don thinks everyone is gay.

"That dad is not gay," I argue. "He's got a mullet and a soul patch."

"Otherwise known as a 'flavor saver.' Gay." Don's adamant. But why does it matter, anyway?

The show always cuts to a shot of a kind, reasonable father, tears streaming down his face, his eyes *begging* to be put out of his misery, having lost his only daughter to a lifestyle worse than your worst nightmare. Then they always say, "And she was such a happy baby!" Every single time. "Cue music!" we both say. The screen then dissolves into a montage of childhood snapshots like the ones in every photo album every parent in the world has of their kids. Every single porn star has a parent somewhere with a photo album of the kid in a onesie with a pacifier in his or her mouth—the same mouth that, eighteen years later, will be jammed by a ten-inch schlong! Probably pierced! Who can I pay to make sure they don't get molested by some neighbor, cousin, or babysitter's boyfriend and then numb the pain by doing heroin, crack, or porn?

"Don. Don. Wake up. What if the kids grow up to do porn?"

Don grumbles, "Doesn't strike me as a problem we can solve in the middle of the night . . ."

I don't let up. "How can we make sure they don't?"

"Well, let's just hope they don't." And he turns back to sleep.

"That's not good enough," I say.

He finally sits up. "Well, will they be relaxed porn stars? Will they be the kind of porn stars that let their boyfriends sleep through the night? 'Cause that won't be so bad."

"'Boyfriend'? I wish! If I were just your boyfriend, I'd be sleeping through the night. I'd be younger, thinner, and I wouldn't be wondering if I'd already ruined our kids with my anxiety. If I'd somehow planted the seed for them to grow into meth whore junkies. Do you think I have, Don? Seriously. Do you think it's too late?"

Don's falling asleep again as he answers. "If it is, let's hope they're the best damn whore junkie porn stars they can be. Right? As long as they do their best . . . And they have health insurance."

Turns out, he's not so much fun to talk to at three a.m.

The next morning, Don is, as always, well rested and chipper and has no recollection of talking me off the ledge in the middle of the night. I'm stressed and exhausted but it's my turn to take the kids to school, so I rally. We're bopping along in the car, listening to some kids' music, and I look back through my rearview mirror and see Eliza kissing Jonah on the forehead. "My baby brother," she says. I want to burst into tears. Nobody can say my kids aren't affectionate and compassionate and polite. What more could a father want? We stop the car and both kids get out, literally skipping to the schoolyard. Anyone can see the other unmistakable truth about them: they're good kids. And they're *happy*!

Deep down I know my kids won't be on a reality show. And if they are, let it be *Project Runway* or *Top Chef* and not some crazy gossipy, scratch-your-eyes-out exploitation show I can't help but watch. I saw one the other night called *Gigolos*, with this poor guy confessing to the camera how he's proud to be a paid "escort" but still hopes his parents aren't watching. Meanwhile he's *agreed* to let camera crews film him with a crazed, man-hating client who's clearly lost her battle with dieting. She insists on locking a device on his penis called a "cock cage" while shoving a wooden spoon up his ass. What must his parents say when they see that?

"Oh, look, honey, Derek is on TV! Oh, shit . . . There's that wooden spoon I've been looking for since Thanksgiving. Um. Hon? Do me a favor? Grab that pillow and hold it over my face until I stop breathing?"

I wonder if Derek knew about Mary and the apples she was bagging. She's probably one of his clients. And he's bagging *her* right now. Wait! Eliza loves apples. That doesn't mean she's going to become Mary, right?

chapter seventeen

Out in the Park

I, like most parents who don't have a backyard, have been taking my kids to the park since they were very little. Often I would run into the L.A. Latin nannies, and over time, thanks to my still-workable Spanish, I became quite a hit with them. And if I showed up in the middle of the day, I was guaranteed to be the only man there. The nannies would hear me speak a little Spanish—for instance, "Hay una mesa de cambiar en el baño?" (*Does the bathroom have a changing table?*)—and there would be smiling and blushing as they'd usher me to another part of the park, where four or five other nannies would be sitting gossiping, pointing, and giggling.

"Qué papi guapo!" I'd hear. I was a *cute dad* in their eyes. And I liked it. I was like a celebrity. While my broken Argentinean Spanish left a lot to be desired, it beat the hell out of most everyone else's desperate attempts to remember a page out of their seventh-grade Spanish books. (*Spanish One*, p. 24: "El aboo-elo ten-eeah largos bee-gohtes, y muchas canas!") I remember seeing a particular mother yelling at her nanny once, pointing to a diaper bag and screaming, "Forgetta the wetta wipes! El niño tiene poopie. Tiene chili con carne en el diaper-o!" Did she really think her hysterical version of

Spanglish was better than just saying "the baby pooped" *slowly* and in English?

I started going to the park more often. I'm not an idiot. If these ladies wanted to treat me like I was Ricky Martin, then I felt it was my duty to deliver them Ricky Martin. Only, you know, Jewish. And older. And with a tight spandex undershirt to hide the love handles. Marisol would be waiting for me on some days with a picnic blanket and a full spread of snacks. Sofia would whip out a Ziploc of cookies she'd made the night before–"gluten-free," she'd announce with a cute accent that reminded me of, well, every single one of my relatives. I'd thank her profusely for her thoughtfulness at remembering my recent diagnosis of Celiac Disease. Then Lupe would pull me in another direction, where she'd uncover a casserole dish "quince minutos a cuatro cincuenta!" (*fifteen minutes at 450 degrees*).

"Daddy!" Eliza would call out, plaintively. She got what was happening and didn't like it. She was my girl and didn't like competing. Jonah, all boy, would dive headfirst into the sand and not come up for air until we were leaving. He liked getting free toys and snacks and didn't care where they came from.

After several months of this, I couldn't help feeling guilty. Not just because of the food, the toys, and the handmade knitted sweater. I felt I was misleading them by flirting as much as I was. I wasn't a *straight* Spanish-speaking dad. I was the other kind. So I promised myself I would tell them the truth, if they asked, that I climbed into bed every night with a muchacho, not a mujer. But for the time being, they weren't asking and I didn't want to disclose more than I needed to, a strategy that until recently seemed to work fine for Ricky Martin. For years he managed to flirt and tease his fans with his charming "maybe I am, maybe I'm not" routine. Even without the twenty-nine-inch waist, I could deliver the same sense of mystery to my nanny fans. *Don't ask, don't tell*—bad for our armed forces, but in the playground? Maybe okay. I'm not proud of it but I was a little afraid of the backlash. I was afraid of what these likely Catholic, Latin American women would think of me. I was disappointed in my willingness to let my shame and fear and love of tamales push me back toward the closet. It was a long journey to become the evolved, proud, self-assured gay man and father that I like to think I am. Just clearly not evolved or proud *enough*.

On the other hand, this was no time to be political. Not when someone was eagerly making me taquitos with guacamole from scratch. And I wasn't actually *lying* to them. I certainly didn't hold back when we all agreed that the park groundskeeper was cute. I figured anyone who could put two and two together knew I was gay. But I was Ricky Martin to them and Ricky Martin's a mo. So I concluded that the truth was known by my noontime novias and didn't have to be said.

Clearly I wasn't that comfortable with the situation, because I cut back on my visits to the park. But then I started to miss my girls. I needed my updates on their lives. They were like my *stories*, my telenovelas. I knew who was married and who was single; who was quitting her job because of a bossy mom whom she'd caught sleeping with someone else and felt uncomfortable with the information; and whose brother-in-law had just been diagnosed with prostatitis.

One day, I was alternating pushes between my two kids on the swings when Lupe came running over to me in tears. I think I actually saw Eliza rolling her eyes, *Here we go again.* Lupe's second cousin, Ramon, was gunned down with his fiancée while coming out of a market in El Salvador somewhere. It was a horrible hit-and-run and police there were looking for the murderer. I couldn't help wondering if maybe they were involved in some shady business Lupe didn't know about. Maybe the culprits knew one or both of them and were getting revenge. I wanted to know more but my Spanish has its limits. I tried to communicate.

"A lo mejor están metidos en algo? O conocen alguien—" (*Maybe they were caught up in something or knew—*) Lupe cut me off, insisting they were innocent victims and not drug addicts. I shook my head. Had I said anything about drugs? I was clearly misunderstood. And I think Lupe felt the same way. She looked at me as though I'd somehow betrayed her by even speculating. I quickly conceded that it was the most horrible way for two people, two *so very innocent* people, to die. She nodded and turned back to her charges. But Lupe looked at me differently from that point on—like I had made an assumption about her and her family because of what had happened. Like I was judging them because they were Latin American. I was just like everyone else, she must've thought, "one of them." I felt bad, because I would have thought the same thing had *anyone* been gunned down like that in broad daylight. I wanted to convince her, but since she never brought it up again, I never knew what she was thinking. I noticed she went missing from the park after that. The others explained to me that she had gone back to

El Salvador for a while. I felt bad about her family's crisis. I wished I'd been able to get that across to her more. At least I still had Marisol and Sofia to talk about it.

• • •

A few weeks later out of the blue, one of the ladies smiled tauntingly and conspiratorially asked me, "Señor Dan, dónde está tu esposa?" (*Where is your wife?*) Ka-boom.

I'd been dreading this moment. I'd hoped they just assumed I was gay, as we all did with Ricky Martin. But as it turned out they didn't know. So now what? If I said, "No tengo esposa. Tengo esposo. Soy gay. Me gustan los mucho macho muchachos!" I was certain of challenging or even offending a demographic that, until then, had been singing my praises and feeding me grapes.

Maybe I should lie, I thought. I could easily tell them my "esposa" is at home. Or at work. Or dead? So what? Who cares? I don't know these women. Whom does it hurt? Okay, I'd be betraying not only my own personal journey to a proud and honest life as a gay man but also I'd be in effect killing Don—or giving him an imaginary sex change. And why? Because the tamales were good? No. I couldn't betray Don and every gay man or woman who risked and sometimes even lost their lives fighting for *my* freedom to even be a father. I turned to Esperanza, who was handing me an empanada made with creamed corn. Wow, she was a good cook. I knew I had to confess, but my mouth was full and suddenly Jonah called me from the top of the play structure to watch him go headfirst down the spiral slide. I ran to catch him: I know his little neck is flexible but wasn't keen to test it. Jonah landed in my arms and I carried him back toward the blankets of El Salvador and Guatemala. Esperanza, Marisol, and the others were focused on their charges. The moment had passed. "We're going to go now! Hasta luego." I had avoided the answer altogether. *They won't even remember.*

Jonah and Eliza and I walked hand-in-hand to the car. Eliza then said, out of the blue, "Those ladies like you, Daddy." Yes, they did. I knew that. And I liked them. Damn. I had to stop. We turned around and headed back.

"Where are we going?" The kids were pulling me and pointing toward the car. They'd already moved on. But I couldn't.

We got back to the blankets and I told the ladies I was in the park by myself today because "mi *esposo* está trabajando," and then I added, "*El* es un escritor" so there would be no mistakes about the gender. The ladies didn't flinch. Then, as if from nowhere, Lupe, apparently just back in the country, piped in with "El es tan guapo como tu?" (*Is he as handsome as you?*) I laughed, blushing a little before responding, "Not even close." They all laughed. I hugged Lupe and told her how much I'd missed her.

"I've been thinking about you," I told her, "and your family. I hope you're okay." She took my hands in hers and thanked me. She told me how much she'd enjoyed getting to know me in the park.

And then she added: "Mi hermano tiene un novio. Ellos quieren tener hijos pero es muy difícil. Les voy a hablar de tu." *(My brother has a boyfriend. They want to have kids but it's very difficult. I will tell them about you.)* I was afraid to speak as the emotion was caught in my throat. Holding back tears, I smiled and nodded and then just gave her a hug before the kids and I headed back to the car.

I'd been an asshole. I had done to all of them exactly what I feared they'd do to me. Fear had kept me from being honest with them, which, in turn, didn't *allow* them the opportunity to show me how open-minded and accepting they really were.

I have no real interest in being a political activist. It's a lot of work and it sounds like that could cut into my TV time. That being said, my life is political by its very nature, and I have to be ready to defend my rights and freedoms at any given moment. When Ricky Martin came out publicly he said he did it because of his kids. He said if he didn't live his life in a completely open and honest way, what message was he sending to them? I guess I have a lot more in common with him than I thought. I love being in a country where I can live as a man, with another man, where we can have kids and be a family. If I don't wear it proudly on my sleeve, I'm only perpetuating the same prejudice I fear. Doesn't matter how easy it may be. Or how much I fucking *love* homemade tamales.

I showed them all a photo of Don next time I went to the park. But not that flattering. I still like being the *guapo* one.

chapter eighteen

The *F* Word

Eliza and I are in a skipping contest coming out of her schoolyard when suddenly she stops short.

"Daddy," she says.

I stop. "What is it, sweetie?"

"That's Tilley," she says, pointing across the street. "Isn't she fat?"

I am stopped dead in my tracks. It's like I've just walked into a wall. But Eliza continues to skip ahead, oblivious to my reaction. I call to her to come back to me. I have to think fast. But I don't have the slightest idea what the hell I'm going to say. She said the *F* word. About another kid. She's in kindergarten, for God's sake; can't "baby fat" stay innocent for a little while longer? At least till first grade? That being said, little Tilley, cherish her, really ain't so little. There's no way around the fact that Tilley's round. Okay, I'll say it: she is fat. If they had a contest to pick the poster child for childhood obesity, she'd win. Or at least place. And this kid sports a perpetual fluorescent orange mustache from the "barbecue-flavored" snacks she's always shoveling into her mouth.

I know. I sound a little mean. Maybe because Tilley is mean. She's the class bully. And it's no wonder. They say kids who bully are often protecting themselves from being teased. I certainly don't want Eliza to play any part in teasing another little kid by calling her fat. Tilley could stand to learn a few things about compassion and kindness and the dearth of nutrition in a bag of nacho-flavored Doritos, true, but girls have enough of a challenge growing up with a positive body image.

I look down at Eliza on the sidewalk. I think to myself, *Time to break the cycle, man! This is your chance!*

I open my mouth, but what the hell am I going to say? What exactly is the correct message? I'm in a tight spot. The simple truth? Tilley *is* fat. Perhaps the lesson is about how kids come in all shapes and sizes. Or maybe I need to say that no kid *wants* to be overweight. I can use this as an opportunity to tell my precious, impressionable daughter that we don't point out particular physical traits about a person because we don't know how that would make them feel. Yes. This seems like the way to go. It's been only a few seconds and yet I'm drowning in uncertainty. I suddenly feel hungry. I need a snack. A bowl of cereal, perhaps. Or a plate of pad Thai. No! A giant black-and-white cookie. Stuff the feelings. That's right. Stuff them right up.

This is my one shot to teach my kid about acceptance and body image and compassion and the importance of good nutrition all at the same time. But no pressure. I simply want the next thing I say to be firm and clear and carry weight, so to speak. Eliza's looking up at me. My stalling is clearly making her anxious. Finally, I squat down and look her squarely in the eyes.

"Eliza, sweetie, let's not ever use the word 'fat' to talk about another person. Okay?"

"Why, Daddy?"

"Well. Different kids process food differently . . ." She looks at me blankly. "Do you know what that means?" She shakes her head.

"It's what happens—I mean, once food gets inside your body, it does stuff—"

"You mean when it turns to poop?" she asks, holding back a laugh.

"Uh, yes. Sort of. When food gets inside your tummy, all the good stuff helps make you healthy and strong. And all the extra stuff we don't need turns into poop. Or it gets stored as fat on your body."

"Oh," she says. I think she's getting it.

"Some kids are small and others are big. But what makes us look different on the outside doesn't mean we're different on the inside. You know?"

She nods. Now she starts looking around. She's bored. But I'm not done.

"Many kids don't *like* the fact that they're heavy but they struggle with it and being called 'fat' could hurt their feelings. We don't want to hurt Tilley's feelings."

Eliza looks away. She's such a compassionate soul, I can tell she feels bad. But then she says, "But Tilley *is* fat. Right, Daddy?" Her eyes are as round and wide as—as a chocolate bundt cake. Oh yeah. That's what would be really good right now. A moist, chocolate bundt cake with a lot of frosting.

I'm not going to lie to my daughter—or make her think she's got vision problems.

"Yes, Eliza. Tilley's a little . . . *heavy*. Let's use that word, but only when we're talking in private, okay?" I hate the word "heavy" and would die if someone used it to describe me. Or "hefty" or "husky"! Eww. But for Eliza's sake, this is going to work.

I continue, "What's way more important is that Tilley is a nice person and you like her."

"Tilley's not that nice," she says. "She's a bully."

"Right. And maybe she is a bully because she doesn't like what people say to her. So . . . let's not ever talk about what Tilley looks like in front of any other kids—and especially not Tilley. Because she punches. Okay?" Eliza nods. I'm relieved. It was probably more than I needed to say, but I never seem to learn moderation. Less is more. Less talk. Less worry. Less chocolate bundt cake.

I look down at Eliza and she's clearly had enough. All right. Moving on. We head toward the car. Eliza is quiet for only a beat.

"What if I like her dress? Can I tell her?" Oh my God. I've completely confused her. I should've kept my fat—oops, I mean *heavy*—mouth shut; told her not to call Tilley "fat" and kept right on walking. By making it a whole thing—trying to tell her how *serious* it is that we not hurt Tilley's feelings—I've taken a highlighter to the whole "fat" issue in her head and stressed her the fuck out. I look at her tiny, confused face.

"Yes, lovey, of course. You can always say something nice to your friends. That would make her feel good." Eliza smiles. We keep on walking.

"But being fat is super bad, right, Daddy?" I close my eyes and die a little bit. Why do I talk? What's wrong with just walking? I don't want Eliza thinking that "fat" is the worst adjective to describe a person either. Even if I, since early in my life, was led to believe otherwise.

• • •

I've never been overweight. But in my house growing up, fat *was* the worst thing you could be. And while my father and mother and sister struggled, I managed to stay a consistent weight for most of my life. But I felt pressure all the time *not* to let it happen to me. And by pressure I mean a death grip.

In my life, food has always had power, both when I've wanted it and when I've wished I hadn't had it. It's always been both reward *and* punishment. You don't eat, you're good. You eat, you're bad. And once you're already bad, you may as well have a second helping. Or a third. You can be good tomorrow. It's a great system if you are looking to cement a lifetime of inner struggle. But wait, there's more! Food, I learned, is an excellent weapon of manipulation as well. That's right, if you order right now, you can project all your own food neurotica onto a friend or loved one absolutely free!

My mom didn't like it when my dad gained weight. And he, in turn, didn't like it when she told him how to eat. She'd buy tempting foods, either consciously or not, perhaps to test his resolve. Or was it a way of testing how much he loved her? But he'd always resent the test, naturally, and eat. She'd glare at him and he'd eat some more, using food to exert his power and control. I could read the thought bubble over his head: *Watch this, lady, I'm having a third ice cream sundae 'cause* nobody *tells me what to do!*

They also had a little system when my mother thought my father was eating too fast. She would tug on her ear. It was supposed to be a subtle, clandestine signal she'd give him when he didn't realize he was shoveling his food. But there was one problem. His face was always down during a scarf-fest, so he couldn't *see* her give him the signal. So it evolved into a loud banging with her elbow to get his attention, along with a loud, sharp *"Julio!"* He'd look up, startled, and she'd tug on her ear. It was about as subtle as Lady Gaga in a bikini with her hair on fire during a halftime show.

Given the attention and power food had when I was growing up, it's no surprise I've been able to pick up a few pointers on how to play the same fucked-up game with myself. I'll have what I want and then kick myself for having it. *What? Chocolate hazelnut donuts? And they're gluten-free? I'll take two!* And then: *No wonder you just tore through the seat of your "skinny" jeans, Fatty, Fatty Bo Batty!*

But after this wonderful sidewalk lesson I've given Eliza, she'd probably tell me not to call myself "Fatty" if I don't want to hurt my own feelings. I'd explain how it's different when I'm the one saying it. And she'd probably want to know why: *Do you want to hurt your own feelings, Daddy?* Hmm. If it would make me lose five pounds, yes.

I know my relationship with food needs to change. We need to maybe take a break from each other. See other people.

When Don and I were expecting Eliza, we talked about our struggles with food and the power it seemed to have over our lives. How we both longed to rid ourselves of these demons, if not for ourselves, for the sake of our kids.

"Let's make sure we never make them feel like some foods are 'good' and some foods are 'bad.'" That was a popular theory. And an admirable goal. But guess what? Some foods *are* bad. And some good. So what kind of bullshit parenting is it when you treat a carrot stick the same as a Nutter Butter? There is only one thing in a carrot—*carrot!* A fucking Nutter Butter has at least a dozen ingredients, most of which are either sugar, oil, or some other ingredient made up of sugar and oil. "Let's not make dessert a reward for eating the rest of the meal," Don said at one point. Okay. Good one. But any parent will tell you that kids *only* want dessert and if they don't *have* to eat their broccoli, they won't. So pretty soon, dinners would be made up of popsicles, pudding, and marshmallow treats.

"Let's not go overboard with all that 'organic' bullshit," we would both agree. It is beyond obnoxious when a parent removes an organic radish, goat's milk yogurt, and a tofu square from a BHP-free plastic container and yells, "Snack time!" Without fail, a bunch of scrappy-looking kids with matted hair and premature body odor appear as if from nowhere, like woodland creatures scurrying out of hollowed tree trunks and mossy knolls. Eagerly they skip with ignorance-is-blissful speed, failing to bat an eye when Mommy whips out her sagging workhorse of a breast, offering a liquid refreshment to her six-, seven- and eight-year-olds. Why? Kids get used to what they know. That is, until one of them gets a whiff of a real Devil Dog or Hostess Sno Ball. Then all bets are off: *Put that tit away, Mom, unless you're willing to wrap it in chocolate and marshmallow and fill it with cream!*

On the other hand, why *should* there be more than twenty-five ingredients in a jar of peanut butter? And why partially hydrogenate oil and infuse it into every food a kid eats? If you *have* to do it, do it all the way! *Fully* hydrogenate that oil. Commit to it. Don't hold back. All or nothing, baby!

Suffice it to say, food has taken up a huge part of my psyche over the past forty years, and even more so since I've become a parent. The stress of my kids' nutrition and my own has taken a toll on me—ironically, in the form of ten extra pounds.

I can't imagine how I'm not passing these food issues and body shame to my kids. They'll pick up on it even if I don't say it out loud. Because—I gotta say this—*I don't want them to be fat!* Sorry. I have to be honest. I also want them to have a healthy relationship to food without feeling guilt or shame or paralyzed by whether a food is good or bad. And while the road to weight gain is so *easy* for a kid—the daily exposure to candy, cupcakes, pizza, and french fries at every turn—the battle for a healthy body image and self-esteem is among the *toughest.*

We were at the local pool and I overheard a parent noticing a heavyish eight-year-old wearing a bikini. Her mother brushed it off with "What can I do? She loves that bathing suit."

The other mother smiled and nodded reassuringly. "Good for her," she said. "Good for her!"

But really? What exactly is so good about it?

Something that still bothers me today is the image of a particular girl, Marcy, at a summer camp I went to. Marcy was overweight and wore bikinis. Her belly stuck out between the two pieces of fabric like marshmallow squeezing out of the s'mores she'd stuff in her face after polishing off the Good Humor ice cream bar that melted into her belly button. I was disgusted by that girl—angered by her. How *dare* she let herself go like that! But it was a crazy reaction to one little girl from an eight-year-old boy. Okay, maybe a little less crazy from a little gay boy, but still. Who cares? She was a kid! I was wrong to have that reaction. Just as I'm wrong to have it now, as a grown-up, trying to rid myself of these weight-obsessed demons.

Eliza got her first bikini at her last birthday party. It was more of a tankini. But *wow*, did she love it. I had mixed feelings about a six-year-old wearing a two-piece. It's panties and a bra, no matter how many seahorses they paint on it. What's next? Little baby thongs and Carter's brand garters? I don't like it. But Eliza wore her tankini to bed, she loved it so much. And she has a fantastically adorable, beautifully perfect tummy and, thank God, has no issue with people seeing it. Her daddy could learn a thing or two about that.

I come down to breakfast a few days after Tilley-gate in a new pair of jeans I'm breaking in. They're a little tight, I admit, but nothing a few deep knee bends won't fix. Eliza bolts down the stairs and looks at me. She doesn't say anything for a few seconds.

"What is it, sweetie?" I ask her.

"Those pants, Daddy."

"Yeah. They're new. You like them?"

She is very deliberate when she says, "You look like you're a little . . . *heavy*."

Now I'm still a gay man and the words hit me like a bullet. It's the kind of bullet that explodes inside and sprays shame and self-hate throughout my body. Eliza smiles at me, proud that she didn't use the *F* word. But I'm afraid that's not good enough.

"You know what, coconut? When you're talking about Daddy, you shouldn't use the word 'heavy' either."

"What word can I use?" she genuinely wants to know.

I take a few seconds and then it comes to me: "Thin!"

chapter nineteen

The Box

Jonah has this new habit. Almost every night, about thirty minutes after we turn out the lights, he'll find some arbitrary object in the house and bring it to us as though we had been looking everywhere for it.

"Here, Daddy, I found it!" he says one night, handing me a container of dental floss and a sock. The next night it's a tape measure. Then it's a battery. One time he brought Don the wallet he'd thought he'd lost, so his little ploy to get out of bed isn't without its benefits.

On one particular night, however, Jonah tiptoed down the stairs holding a small cardboard box. He kept staring at it as though willing it to be filled with Legos or Skittles.

"Daddy. Guess what I found?" he whispered, handing it to me sleepily. I didn't recognize it but I showed my boy the appropriate gratitude and walked him back to bed. Eliza sleeps in the same room with him and she, of course, was awake.

"What's in the box, Daddy?" she asked. It was already 9:30 and I was starting to get annoyed that both my kids were wide-awake.

"I don't know, sweetie. I haven't really figured it out yet."

I didn't want to switch on the light, so I used a flashlight to examine every side. Finally, I noticed on the bottom a small stamp that read "TLC Pet Hospital." Oh. This was the box that held our dog's ashes. I sighed deeply as I searched for an appropriate explanation at this late hour.

"It's Basia, guys. Remember I told you that after she died, we got to keep her ashes? These are her ashes." Silence.

Eliza was the one to explain it all to her brother. She loves being an expert. On anything. Especially on matters I spend a lot of time explaining to her first. She gets very intense and specific and preachy. I love it.

"Jonah. Basia was very, very old and so she couldn't live anymore. So she died. And after she died, they turned her body into fairy dust and we have it in the box. It's a special box. And we can keep it forever. It's a box only for things that are dead."

"I'm going to die one day," Jonah announced proudly.

"Not for a long, long, long time," I added immediately.

"That's right," Eliza assisted me, "first Papi will die. Then Daddy, then me, and then you. Because you're the youngest. I'm older. So I will die first. And then you can decide where to bury me." That was all I really wanted to hear on that topic. I mean, who wants to consider their own kids' mortality? Not me. Not when I was just getting excited about the two episodes of *Top Chef* I had backed up on my TiVo downstairs.

"Nobody is dying for a long, long time. Tomorrow I'm making pancakes. It's going to be a great day. Now everyone go to sleep!" I kissed them both and slipped out. They were asleep before I hit the door.

I started to head downstairs holding that box in my hands. But I was suddenly reminded of another box I had stuck in the back of my closet over three years ago. I turned back and went into my bedroom closet and pulled everything out onto the floor. There it was: The Box.

It was still sealed from when I sent it from my mother's apartment the summer after my dad died. My mom and sister and I were going through all his things and that box was earmarked for me. It arrived at my house about a week later and I stuffed it in the back of the closet—out of sight both literally and metaphorically. Until some hypothetical day in the future when I would hypothetically feel ready to deal with it—hypothetically. And this wasn't it. Pulling The Box from the closet was just about as much as I could handle for that day.

• • •

It's August and the kids are running naked through the sprinklers. They have only one more week before Eliza starts first grade and Jonah starts his second year of preschool. I can't believe how quickly time has flown. My dad died in March of 2007. Eliza was only two and Jonah wouldn't be born for another six months.

Both kids are a little sunburned from the week we just spent in Cape Cod. My parents used to take us to the Cape during our summers. My dad loved being on the beach. When my kids were picking oysters along the shore of the bay, I remembered doing the exact same thing with him. He'd open them right in front of us, squeeze a few drops of lemon, and suck those gnarly slugs right down. It was gross but we'd laugh.

Lately, I've been seeing his face every time I look at myself in the mirror. So the caulking on my memories of him is beginning to peel away. (Why am I using a home improvement metaphor? I only watch those shows on HGTV because of the before-and-afters they do at the end. And that's only because I love a good makeover show.)

My dad had a playful, passionate quality and the desire to extract the best out of life, like squeezing the most succulent of oranges or brewing an exquisite, robust cup of espresso. I see this quality in myself and hope it catches on to my kids. It's painful to think he'll never get the chance to see them grow into whatever it is they're becoming—their own "makeovers." He won't get to see those subtle but unmistakable ways they'll remind him of me—or of himself. It's too sad to think about. It's no wonder I've felt the need to keep him away—in a box. Maybe it's because I lost a parent so soon after becoming one. The role of "Dad" used to be only his. Then, briefly, it was his *and* mine. Now, just mine.

When I told him I was gay, I don't think my dad ever imagined I'd have kids. That's the one thing that always brought my parents to tears. "It's such a hard life being gay," my mother would say. Well, yeah. Sure, it was hard. But growing up *is* hard. Everyone has their challenges. And fortunately, with the help of trailblazers like Ellen and *Will and Grace* and Dan Savage and *Modern Family*, my dad was around long enough to see me create a "modern family" of my own. He witnessed my relationship with Don for over a decade and watched us develop into a couple that supported each other, shared our lives, building a foundation that tricked us into believing we were prepared to become parents. He had years to develop a healthy relationship with his son-in-law—eventually comfortable enough to argue with him one instant and laugh with him another. Don also laughed *at* him but that never went over so well. My dad was always a little oversensitive. Not in small part because he was a small man. He was maybe five three. And that was on a high hair day. So he wasn't so much into the teasing. But it's hard to take seriously a short little guy whose pants are hiked up in a perpetual "mamel toe," squishing up his junk like a frog trapped in a jar.

Lately, thought, I've been feeling an oddly comforting connection to my dad. I find myself chasing the kids around the house, the way he did with me. Singing to them in the car in weird voices or made-up dialects. Or trying to tickle them under their chin—what my dad used to call "skifu la canaruzi." It doesn't actually mean anything, but I run around saying it. A lot. I am reminded mostly of myself at their age, however, when my kids put on a show. Or try to.

The shows are quite pathetic, really. No structure. No real text. Musically lacking and surprisingly unrehearsed, these shows demonstrate an immaturity in narrative. That's theater-critic-speak for "They suck." But I can't get enough of them. Every time I hear Eliza shout "Ladies and gentlemen," I drop what I'm doing and run for a good seat. Never mind that she hasn't realized there are only gentlemen in this theater. It's not for me to say. I'm on their turf now. Eliza barks orders at her brother to dance and jump and sing "Do Re Mi," which he dutifully attempts with as much flourish as the tough little macho tyke can muster. Poor kid, not remotely blessed with a gay gene.

I think back to the countless shows I used to force my parents to watch. A blanket hung almost perpetually over the chin-up bar crammed into my door jamb (sadly, the only purpose it served). "Ladies and gentlemen," I'd sing out, as I'd hit the play button on the opening number of *A Chorus Line*: "Step, kick, kick, leap, kick, touch!" And I would. All around my room. But not before extorting a buck from Mom and Dad, warning them there would be "no refunds or exchanges." Ah yes, even then my gay gene was working overtime along with the one that kept a keen eye on box office receipts.

I sit and wait while Eliza and Jonah have a quick conference in the middle of their show, which is about a kitty and a friendly rattlesnake that likes popcorn. I wonder if this is how my dad felt as he waited for my extravaganzas to begin. In this moment we're connected: I'm him and my kids are me.

I feel the emotion catch in my throat as Eliza and Jonah begin to sing, and I stuff it back down. I clap and holler for them, delighted by their own pride and enthusiasm. No, I think, this is about the purity of their creative joy. It's no time to sink into sadness. I haven't wanted to explore my feelings about his death since that night in March 2007. Why? I don't know. It's not like there was much between us that went unsaid. I knew he loved me. I knew he was proud. He'd written me plenty of letters over the years where he'd said it outright. In one letter in particular, after I'd already moved to California and was living with Don, he closed by saying, "I love you, Danny. And when I grow up, I want to be just like you." Why, then, I ask myself, am I so reluctant to explore the memories—or open the box?

I think The Box has taken on a kind of epic power. As though I'm hoping it represents everything about him and the love he felt for me. Or perhaps I fear it won't have any resonance at all. I know I'm worried it's going to remind me of the last months of his life. Those were the months when I struggled to be strong for my then two-year-old daughter as she recovered from the heart surgery, while I watched my father's illness destroy every recognizable quality he ever had.

My father got sick in September of 2005. Eliza was only six months old and my parents had just come out to spend a week with us. We celebrated my dad's seventy-first birthday at a restaurant near Santa Barbara ironically named Lucky. Eliza sat in his lap and ate her first bites of solid food. It was nice to see my dad hold her, nuzzle her, or as our birth mom, Monica, might say, "love on her."

Three days before my fortieth birthday, I was coming out of the gym and had four messages on my cell phone. I quickly learned that my dad was going in for emergency surgery after being diagnosed with a brain tumor. It was called a glioblastoma or, if you didn't want to use the clinical or medical term, you could call it what doctors did: "the Terminator." Cute, huh? Why cancer needs a nickname, I don't know. They gave him eighteen months.

The first year went by quickly. He had his surgery. Did radiation. And a successful nine-month treatment with a chemo pill, which allowed him to enjoy almost the same quality of life he had before: he traveled, he ate, he exercised. And most of all, he vowed to beat the odds. He refused to accept the possibility he could be dying. My dad's strength and will were remarkable. I kept hoping it was something he'd passed along to me.

It was during that year we tried to visit my parents with Eliza as much as we could. They came out to L.A. a few times to see us as well. But then, a year later, on his seventy-second birthday, the tumor came back and they had to operate again. This was the beginning of what became the longest and most painful chapter: waiting for the end. It felt like it was happening in slow motion. First came the loss of memory; then his hearing and eyesight failed; and then he lost his ability to walk. But in reality, in relation to the rest of his life, it all happened at lightning speed. From November to February, parts of him just disappeared, like puzzle pieces that go missing until you can no longer make out an image. We kept trying to remind him of things. Show him pictures. Make him laugh. But brain cancer has this ruthless way of erasing the functioning of a person—one bit at a time. Like a python, the brain tumor takes hold of its victim and sadistically squeezes the life out of him: his agility, dexterity, speech, memory, humor, continence . . . eventually all identifiable signs of his personality, until there's virtually nothing left. There was no contest, really, given the magnitude of our opponent's arsenal, but my dad never surrendered. He never gave in. He continued to tell us he was "fighting it" even in a wheelchair, with barely a voice left and a faraway look in his eyes. Looking back, I felt both punished and proud of his resolve. Punished, I admit, for selfish reasons. I desperately wanted to have one more conversation with him before his mind evaporated. I wanted to hear him tell me he knew what was happening, and he was okay. I wanted him to offer me words of encouragement and advice, words to take with me forward, in his absence. Words spoken man to man, father to son, and from one dad to another.

I remember the day Don and I told him we were expecting another baby and we wanted to name it after him. It felt important to let him know that there was a new life coming into our lives at a time when we were clearly losing another. He seemed to take this in. But I can't ever be sure.

I never imagined, when we had Eliza, that her grandfather, her "abuelo," was someone she'd meet a mere *ten times* in her life. That he would become someone she and Jonah would know only through stories and photos. It was the same way I had learned about my grandfathers, who had both died by the time I was two. We have a little book of photos of Eliza taken with my parents, and she used to love to flip through it when she'd be sitting in her car seat. I'd look into the rearview mirror and say, "That's your abuelo!"—trying desperately to make it stick somewhere deep inside her. So she'd know how much he loved her. So she'd know *something* about him. I knew I'd be doing that a lot with the kids until they both recognized him on their own.

But what about him could I pass along to my kids either consciously or not? With adopted kids, I couldn't help wondering how my father could become a part of them. Maybe he wouldn't. Or maybe something about the kind of parent I've become, passed on to me from him, would naturally be passed on to them? I could only hope.

As the days crept toward the inevitable, my feelings about both my daughter and my dad were so raw. I wasn't used to feeling this exposed. Loving them both so completely, unconditionally, and vulnerably was scary. It almost didn't feel natural, really, to be so open and unprotected. But it was much bigger than me. Bigger than all of us. I think my succumbing to the reality that he was dying was part of nature's plan.

I was never very physical with my father. But over those last three months I found myself hugging him when I had the chance. Kissing him on the cheek or the forehead. A hand massage. A foot massage. I'd clip his nails or rub his shoulders, far more intimate than I'd ever imagined being with him. But things were different. He'd just look up at me, at all of us, so helplessly. The way Eliza looked up at us from the moment she could focus her eyes.

"It's going to be okay," I'd say to him—the way I'd say it to Eliza—as I'd tuck him in. I'd feed him, just as he had fed Eliza those first few bites on his seventy-first birthday. He seemed to take comfort in having me there with him as he ate. The care I gave him felt like something primal. Dare I say, maternal?

But he never stopped being my dad. And I know he kept reminding himself of that fact. One time, he turned to the nurse who'd been living there for over a month and managed to whisper to her, "That's my son."

"I know, Julio." She smiled at him sympathetically. "I know your son."

His response? "I just like to say it."

I was his son. He was my father. I was Eliza's father. But oddly, my role had become the same in both their lives. You see adult diapers on the shelves at the store not far from the baby ones. But it doesn't really sink in, until you're living it. And that's when it sank in for me—the first time I saw my dad wearing a diaper, needing to be changed. And me, averting my eyes out of respect.

He'd hate me to see him this way, I'd think. But he didn't even notice because he wasn't there anymore.

I had always prayed I'd get through most of my life without ever having to see my father naked. You know, beyond the accidental glimpse in a public bathroom or passing by his bedroom at some point in my life. But honestly, what's the big deal? It's a penis. Okay, I said it. I was beyond the awkwardness now, wasn't I? No. Because it didn't matter what it was called. I didn't want to see it. Not when it was my father's.

But there he was, lying on his bed. Half-asleep. And I was the only one there to help change him. Deep breaths. It can't be worse for me than it is for him, right?

"It's going to be okay," I told him, or I told myself. And it was. And I got over it. I got over all of it. Time to grow up. This is what it is. Call it by its name. It's a "penis." And this is "dying."

My dad passed away a few weeks later, in his sleep, with all of us by his side. It was time. The few days before his death, Eliza kept entering his room. I'd pick her up and she'd stare at my father. Almost knowingly. I couldn't have gotten through it without her. She was a tiny, bright light in the darkest of tunnels. So much life in her. And strength. And humor. She'd lay a little Kleenex down on the bed and ask you to rest your head on it. And just before you'd make contact, she'd pull it away and laugh. A prankster. Just like me. And just like my dad. When he got sick and he quite literally lost what power he had left, his worst nightmare had come true. Not that he was dying—that's everyone's nightmare of course—but that he'd become small. Smaller than ever before.

The irony, looking back, is that my father was always quite *big*. He had a great personality, loads of charisma, and a big presence. He loved the act of leading, teaching, inspiring, supporting, and encouraging. It's how he was with me. I remember when he taught me to drive. He couldn't wait for us to get out there and begin his signature, six-month intensive lesson plan. First day, lesson one. He drove me out to a giant parking lot, parked the car, we both got out, and I got into the driver's seat. He told me to turn on the ignition. I did. He told me to turn off the ignition. I did. He opened the car door and got out and told me to do the same. Lesson one was over. I was furious but I learned how to drive that way. In fact, I learned a lot as a result of his thorough and patient manner. Look at that. He was a pretty damn good coach after all.

• • •

The next morning, after I made the pancakes, the kids asked me where I put the box of our dog's ashes. Together we chose a spot on the mantel by their trophies and dioramas. It was in that moment that I made a decision.

"Come on, guys, I want you to help Daddy with something." The kids skipped up the stairs with me and into my bedroom. I dragged The Box out of my closet and into the middle of the floor. I told them it was a box of treasures left by their abuelo. Their eyes widened, a mix of excitement and a little nervousness at the mystery and reverence of it all. I told them I wanted them there for support but also as an opportunity to tell them a little about him. I showed them a photo of him. Jonah looked at it and at me.

"That's your daddy?" I nodded. "And he's dead?" I know the notion of daddies being able to die is stressful for them. They're not the only ones.

I impressed upon them that "Abuelo was very old and very sick. And I'm not going to die for a very, very long time." I said it so my words could be imprinted in their minds, and hopefully into Fate itself. But they were not thinking about that.

"Will you make a box of prizes for us when *you* die?" Eliza asked. She was after more swag. Typical.

"Yes, monkey." I laughed. *Is nobody upset that Daddy is dead in this little scenario?* "I will make you guys a box with so many wonderful things." There was a beat. Eliza looked to Jonah, then back to me.

"Maybe you'll die before Papi?" I didn't like where this was going.

It was a good time to turn back to the box, which, as it turned out, was something of a time capsule, or a *human* capsule of sorts—a catalog of various aspects of my dad's personality.

First, a bunch of business cards in a little leather holder. I immediately smiled, because my dad always seemed to put the cart before the horse and get cards printed each time he found a new way of defining his career. "Julio Bucatinsky. Systems Strategist and Counselor" read one. "Julio Bucatinsky. Management Coaching" read another. No wonder when I was ten years old and my dad encouraged me to become a magician, I made "The Great Houdanni" business cards before I ever learned to palm a coin. Eliza wanted to keep this one. I pulled out the cards and handed her the little wallet. I imagined my six-year-old's business cards, printed in pink, of course. What would they say? "Eliza Bucatinsky. Making bubbles underwater since 2005."

The second item in the box was a stack of notebooks, each with writing only on the first page. The rest were blank. He had wanted to be a writer more than anything else. I often feel an odd twinge of pride and guilt that I've been able to fulfill that particular dream. I turned to the first page of one of the notebooks and was immediately startled by how just the sight of his handwriting seemed to bring him back. I could hear his voice.

The third item in the box was a small netted bag of three cloth balls. A juggling kit. Jonah picked them up. "Look! Abuelo put something in the box for us!"

I swallowed hard. "Yes, Jonah. He wanted you to have those." Jonah immediately pulled the balls out of the bag and dropped them down his shirt. Just like I used to do when I was a kid.

Next, I found a leather satchel I had bought for him when I was in Italy shooting *Under the Tuscan Sun*. I only now remember buying the beautiful messenger bag, a writer's bag, really, for my dad. I never imagined it would turn up in my hands again. In one of the pockets of the bag, another business card: "TechMar Consulting Group." My dad was the only one in the "Group" but that didn't stop him.

Eliza reached for the last item in the box. It was a multicolored hammock. Folded up. My dad loved tying it between two trees to create a quiet, personal space for him to read or think or smoke a cigar. The kids asked me to put the hammock up in their bedroom. There was no way that would ever work.

I immediately said yes.

chapter twenty

Let's All Do the Twist

I'm in the kitchen with Eliza and she's playing a pinball game on my iPad to distract herself as I comb out the knots she accrued in her bed last night. I blew off giving her a shower and shampoo after our day at the beach. Bad call. Eliza has fine hair that's very, *very* blond. And a day at the beach means it gets gnarly with sunscreen, sand, and possibly a hermit crab or two.

"Ow," she screams every three or four minutes, "Daddy, stop!" I hate how it hurts her but also suspect she's developed a penchant for the dramatic from the guy who's holding the comb. Regardless of the struggles, I usually enjoy this time with her each morning. When we're not in a hurry it can actually be quiet and intimate, my left hand on her head, the other moving slowly through the strands of hair. But it's also a tenuous balance to carefully avoid a snag, which is like stepping on a land mine in an otherwise tranquil forest. At long last, the knots are out and her hair is ready for styling. And there's nothing *not* fun about a full head of blond hair waiting to be sculpted into a style, clipped, tied, or braided.

What is it about gay men and doing hair? Yes, it's a cliché and a stereotype, which means there's truth in it. But I would no sooner allow myself to be defined by my proclivity for liking a cute hairstyle than I would by my proclivity for sleeping with a man. They are among many truths about myself that I'm happy to own rather than deny. Among all the other reasons we were happy to be having a girl, we also knew we'd get to realize a childhood dream: long, silky hair of our very own to brush!

Not every hairdresser is gay. And of course, not every gay person is a hairdresser. That being said, I'd venture to say *most* of us notice hair. We have an opinion about it, whether it's a particularly cute coif or a hot, ratty mess. If the eyes are the windows to the soul, then hair is the set of drapes. So when the hair equation includes two dads, their six-year-old blond daughter, and a bottle of detangler, the battle for the comb is inevitable.

I hear Don coming down the stairs. I'd better hurry, because he loves doing our daughter's hair even more than I do and is likely to rip the comb from my hand. He's a master of the comb-out and I tend to be the style guy. But I've hijacked the comb this morning and pray I've gotten away with it. I pull the sides of her hair together in the back and start braiding it.

"Looks cute," Don says. He means it. But there's also a look in his eye that says, *Lucky bitch, how'd you get to her before I did?* Don dips a comb in some water and starts working it through our son's hair. Jonah's is short. He's a boy. So he's done in about four seconds. I pretend not to gloat that I got to Eliza before he did. He pretends not to care. But he does. And I do. Way too much.

When I was a kid, I used to put my footie pajamas on my

head and pretend to have a mane of golden hair cascading down my back. I'd flip it with my hand the way I saw Cher doing on her variety show. My laid-back, hippie parents tried to take the free-to-be-you-and-me approach and allowed me to dance around the house "tossing my salad" this way and that—but I could tell they were concerned. They wanted me to learn to love the hair I had. Or maybe they were just embarrassed when they had company over and I'd offer to let them twist my pj's into a chignon. Don once told his Irish Catholic mother he wanted to be a hairdresser when he got older and she promptly explained how his only chance of *getting* older would be never to mention such a ridiculous idea again. But that didn't stop him from wishing for a head of princess hair he could style as his very own. That and a deluxe Julie Andrews scrapbook. A guy's got to dream, huh?

If only we could spend more time doing the things we gays like to do rather than scrutinizing ourselves, criticizing and defending our choices—to be a hairdresser or designer or opera buff or flight attendant. (Actually, I don't get that one. I hate to fly. I hate being in a confined space with so many strangers coughing and farting. And get your own damn pillow—what do I look like?)

So. We're gay dads. And we like doing our daughter's hair. There are worse things fathers could do. Right? Well, for Don it actually may be the worst thing he could do. The other day, I discovered him snipping away at Eliza's bangs with a pair of pruning shears. Or was it a nail clipper? It may as well have been a butter knife!

Stop! What are you doing? You'll ruin her! I wanted to say. But he seemed so happy—playing beauty shop with his daughter.

I instead picked my eyeballs off the floor and placed them back in my head and went about my business. When he was done, he stood back to admire his work. Well, it was less "admire" and more "assess damage."

"What do you think?" he asked. Brave of him to ask my opinion. I averted my eyes as long as humanly possible and finally allowed them to find their way to my daughter's head. There it was—bangs like the toothy grin of a jack-o'-lantern or a row of piano keys, alternating long and short, resting on her forehead like a tattered dust ruffle.

"Cute!" I said, poorly masking my horror. He shrugged, acknowledging the mediocrity of the job.

"It'll grow back," I said, less for his benefit than my own.

"Maybe you can take her in to have it cleaned up," he suggested. I was glad it was his idea rather than mine. I nodded. We're here and queer, loud and proud, but we also possess eyes and the good sense to know when to admit defeat and turn our daughter's hair, our playground, over to an actual hairdresser—probably a gay one. Please God, a gay one. We are the best at it after all.

chapter twenty-one

Keeping Up with the Bergmans

It was right in the middle of Monica's pregnancy with Eliza when Don and I were invited to dinner with friends of Don's family, Marguerite and Phil Bergman. They have three kids. Don and I, seeking guidance, were on the lookout for a parenting guru, and Marguerite struck us both as a truly admirable matriarch. An immigrant from Spain who worked in publishing and volunteered in her community, she still found time to make her family a priority. Her husband, Phil, was also a total catch. A creative guy and an authoritative father, Phil commands respect without sacrificing his more tender, loving, and supportive qualities. He's also really funny and good-looking. Too good to be true. Which is why, of course, Don's convinced he's gay. Oh, and their kids? Amazing! They're talented, confident, studious, ambitious, and *love* their parents so much they can't get enough of them. They are affectionate and look at their parents with appreciation and awe, gratitude and devotion. *What's wrong with them?* was my first thought. I kept looking for the cracks but there were none. The family was perfect!

Driving home from the dinner, I was in a sulk in the passenger seat. Don asked me what was wrong. I didn't even know how to put it into words without sounding whiny.

"I'm sad," I admitted, "because Phil and Marguerite aren't my parents."

"No. They're not," Don said with a smile.

"Just seems unfair, that's all. Plus I'll never *be* them. Which really sucks. I'll never be the kind of parents they are."

Don reassured me. "Sure you will. You'll be a great parent."

"Thank you," I said, "but I wasn't saying that so you would—whatever. I'm not saying I won't be a good parent. I'm sure I'll be, you know, fine. I'll just never be *those* parents."

"Okay. No argument there," Don conceded. "You won't *have* those parents and you won't be those parents. Now what?" He looked at me. "You're also never going to be a kangaroo." He laughed. I didn't.

"Shut up," I said. But he didn't.

"And you're never going to be Robert De Niro. Or Snoop Dogg. Or Charlie Brown. Or a potbellied pig. Or an artichoke."

"I'm going to choke you in a minute," I said, laughing.

"You're you. That's it. Cards we're dealt." Of course, he's right. But I can't let it go.

"That's what I mean. The minute you look at someone else's cards—"

"Otherwise known as cheating," he says, cutting me off. I ignore him.

"And you see that ace and that jack, when you're a pair of sixes—"

"That's what you think you are? A pair of sixes? You need more therapy." He's not wrong.

"No. Better than sixes, maybe. I don't know. A ten and an ace," I say.

"I'm the ace," he says confidently. I envy how little Don worries about these things.

"Okay. Fine," I say. "But I want a pair of jacks. Or kings . . ."

"Wanting to be something you're not," he says smugly. "Slippery slope." And then he hits me with an uncharacteristic dose of glass-half-full: "How do you know you're not going to be dealt *another* ten, or another ace? You could be working on four of a kind and you don't even know it." I begin to hear his point. "Maybe even better than the Bergmans," he offers. I smile. Love him.

"You're right," I say. "Nothing wrong with the Bergmans serving as my inspiration. Right? Good to have a role model."

As hard as I might aspire to the Bergman standard of parenting, from the second our beautiful baby was put in my arms, I started questioning my every move. We all do: from the position of their heads in the crib to the kind of formula to buy and eventually to the school you're willing to sell your possessions to pay for and blow anyone you have to in order to get your child admitted. You are forced to make decisions about your children's lives even though there's always the nagging thought that there may be a better way to go.

What's more, we stand by our way of doing things and spout our ideas as dogma to anyone who'll listen. What's the alternative? Admitting we're fucking up our kids? No way. It's maddening to think our parents' generation could possibly have been so smug about their parenting techniques when they had none. On the other hand, we probably have too many! We scrutinize and analyze every detail of our kids' lives—safety-checking and baby-proofing every corner of their environment. Every rough surface or sharp edge in my house has had or may soon have a rubber sleeve, or a beeping alarm around it. I'd go to any lengths to protect my kids from pain. (Or am I protecting myself from worry?) But what does it teach them? That every road they take will be paved for them? I don't want that. Marguerite and Phil told us to read *The Blessing of a Skinned Knee*, which is an amazing resource for ways to stop hovering over kids and to teach them self-reliance. Ironically, it's how many of our mothers and fathers parented—but more out of cluelessness than out of a conscious philosophy.

I see the benefits of letting kids face risks and challenges on their own. But the world feels scarier today than when I was a kid. It's not, though. We just know more.

When I was Eliza's age, my friend and I walked home from first grade at P.S. 75 on Ninety-Sixth Street in upper Manhattan, without the help of an adult. Around the same time, I remember being handed a flyer by my teacher on my way home. No, it wasn't a show-and-tell schedule like I just saw in my daughter's backpack. It was a police composite sketch of a serial killer named Charlie Chop-off who was on the loose in the fall of 1972. He was abducting little boys and cutting off their penises. Nice, huh? *Sleep tight!*

I remember telling Don about Charlie Chop-off and he had a hard time believing it was real. "That didn't happen. It was probably just one of those urban myths. And you all got sucked into the drama." I would've gotten annoyed if I hadn't feared he might be right. So I went to my computer and checked on Wikipedia and lo and behold, there it was: "Charlie Chop-off." And apparently they never caught the guy!

So, what do I do? I try to resist my first impulse to monitor my kids' every move. They don't need a chaperone to go upstairs to find their sweatshirt or get a cup of water or go to the bathroom. Well, actually that's a tricky one. The kids are old enough now to step into a bathroom and take care of business on their own. But for years, both kids would come into a men's room with me to go potty, regardless of who else was in there. It got a little dicey as Eliza got older and we'd go into the locker room at the swimming pool. It's only natural I felt the impulse to shield her eyes from the cavalcade of cock swinging in her direction. *Coming through!* I'd want to say. *Innocent eyes are coming through. Put it away!* But it was a men's room after all. Was I being overprotective? Maybe. It's just a human body. Kids need to learn that it's all beautiful. No. Wait. What's happening? Some huge, very old, very naked, and *not* beautiful man is now squatting in front of the kids telling them both how they remind him of his grandkids. I can only pray their eyes don't catch sight of the fossilized ball sac grazing against the floor between his legs.

After considerable tears, and a call to Marguerite Bergman for backup, Eliza agrees to use the ladies' room by herself as long as I promise to stand at the door and wait. She goes in. I try not to get sentimental about this being her "first time" and "my little girl's growing up." Instead I stare at my watch, trying to figure out how long I wait before I need to intervene. A few women come out.

"Did you see a little blond girl in there?" I ask one of them. I wonder whether this woman's washed her hands. So many of the guys don't.

"Oh, she's so cute. In the stall all by herself. Humming! She's darling." And she goes. I smile to myself. *That's my girl!*

A minute or so later, I open the door to the bathroom and call out, "Eliza? You okay?"

"Yes, Daddy."

I want to remind her to wipe but I decide to let that go. More time passes. *Where the hell is she?* I open the door and try and whisper loudly, "Eliza? Are you going poopie? Do you need help?" She can't hear me. But another woman enters, asking if I want her to go check. I decline. I want Eliza to feel the sense of accomplishment at having done it all by herself. If, in fact, she survives to see it happen.

A good five or six minutes later, Eliza emerges from the bathroom.

"I got locked in, Daddy." She's smiling. Why is she smiling?

"You did? You poor thing. Why didn't you call me?"

"I figured out how to squiggle out underneath. I crawled on the floor." My mind flashes to the germs and bacteria undoubtedly having a rave on her knees and elbows. "I washed my hands," she reassures me, "and I came out all by myself!" Okay. Now I really do have to choke back a tear. She did it. Could I have gone in there to help her? I guess so. But I'm glad I didn't.

I think even Marguerite Bergman would agree that the single most important job we have as parents is to *love* our kids unconditionally and to delight in them and let them see that delight. What else? We know not to let them eat rat poison or stand in traffic or say "fuck off," no matter how much we want them to "use their words." Even the best of parents, I realize, let their kids face a challenge or two without supervision or some other safety net. Sure, walk to school by yourself. And good for you, navigating a public restroom on your own? Call it the blessing of the sticky lock! There's nothing quite like the feeling of pushing past your fears.

Okay. I admit it. After two days of internal struggle, I called the swim club and had them oil the bathroom locks. Sue me.

chapter twenty-two

You Are Who You Meet

As soon as the kids were old enough to go to school, we knew we had to branch out from the Bergmans. Entering a school community is like walking through a shopping mall of parenting styles. Fortunately, the kids have landed at one of the best schools in Los Angeles. It's not only a dynamic and innovative learning environment, it has an amazingly diverse and open-minded community of faculty, students, and parents. But getting here was a journey. Jonah was at a different school before this one. And Eliza tried two different preschools and even spent four months at a school in New York City when we were there for work. Each had its challenges. But there was no challenge greater than the first day of school.

At first, the kids cried when we dropped them off. It tore me to pieces. I'd go back to my car, almost in tears myself, and call my sister for support. And we didn't know any of the other parents yet. We were nervous. We didn't know if or how we would fit in. The experience took me back to a feeling I haven't had since childhood.

I'm sure it's not like this for everyone, but for me, there was a definitive moment when I realized I was different from everyone else on the planet. It struck me like a bolt of lightning. The way one might be struck with an "uh-oh" feeling waking up, say, in the midst of the White House State Dinner wearing Superman Underoos with a pee stain in the crotch. That's the feeling I had as a child. At what moment? I remember it like it happened seven minutes ago: me skipping happily up to a group of other five-year-old boys playing on the playground and asking if they all wanted to get naked and play monkey. Um, they didn't. And I became consumed by that "uh-oh" Underoos feeling I haven't been able to shake ever since.

Needless to say, when Don and I showed up to our first meet-and-greet, I was consumed by that nervous, pee-stain feeling right away. Granted, I knew better than to ask any of the other parents to play naked monkey. Before too long we realized we were actually at a wonderful buffet of interesting people, some of whom were also same-sex parents, but all of whom seemed to share our fears and frustrations. It instantly made us feel less alone. I soon found a nice circle of new friends and acquaintances. We'd chat during pickups or drop-offs, even exchange the names of dance teachers or speech therapists over a cup of coffee. In fact, all of them seemed to be warm, smart, open-minded people who gave us a real sense of community. We all seemed to be in the same boat, and yet it was sometimes hard for me to keep my eyes on my own page: "Hmm, that lunch box looks like it keeps food fresher." "I heard karate builds discipline." "What's an auditory processing delay?" "Where does Iris take hip-hop?" "Is Robbie reading? Already? What's your secret?"

I was hyperaware of what everyone else was doing, especially at that first preschool in New York. It's no wonder I started mentally putting all the parents into little categories to help me cope with all the crowd noise:

The WORKING MOM. A busy, multitasking professional who races into school with her kids, an earpiece connected to her BlackBerry on which she's simultaneously texting her assistant while trying to sound insightful on a conference call with London. So she'll occasionally pipe in with "as long as we're all on the same page," while intermittently wiping dried yogurt off the mouth of her daughter, who has a name like Hunter or Clem. She wears twelve-hundred-dollar shoes and tinted glasses to hide the circles under her up-till-three-prepping-for-the-conference-call eyes. She has a kick-ass body and effortlessly gets down on one knee, careful not to rip her Armani pencil skirt, kisses her child goodbye, and repeats "I love you" seven or eight times to alleviate the guilt she feels about working so much.

The AT-HOME DAD. Everyone's pal, this guy shows up to school in his workout clothes and hangs out to talk with all the parents, a few teachers, and the school principal, with whom he has a whole library of private jokes. His kids stay wrapped around his legs as he walks them, literally, to class. He showers them with love and kisses before sending them into the teachers' care—but not before disclosing the special surprise he included in each of their lunch boxes: "I made brownies!" He hangs out after the kids are in class to watch them through one-way mirrored windows—and to flirt with the moms. He's usually pretty good-looking, though he sports an ever-growing midsection from the post-bedtime wine and midmorning brownies he devours while watching internet porn. Oh, and there's always a dab of glitter glue stuck in his hair.

The DOTING MOM. These moms are either stay-at-home or part-timers who put their full-time careers on hold to be there for their kids. They are nervous, eager, and controlling of every move their children make. They sacrificed way too much for parenthood to end up with a kid who loses brain function from a scooter ride with no helmet. They do homework with the kids and sometimes *for* them and schedule dozens of after-school activities they hope will put them on track for the Ivy League. The kids often have some attachment issues with these moms, who insist on staying in the classrooms until their babies stop crying. Outside the class, they often solicit your opinion about their children. ("Does Winnie seem sad to you? She's coloring by herself. Look at her lips. Is that a smile? It's a smile, right?") They'll try anything to help ease their anxiety until four hours have passed and they can take another flake off a Xanax.

The PERFECT/CRAFTY MOM. She is at school every single day and always looks damn good. She's crunchy/glamorous in her Dansko clogs, giant gold hoop earrings, and vintage Marimekko handbag. She used to have a great figure but hasn't yet lost the paunchy baby weight. She's got a great smile and knits extraordinary cashmere sweaters by hand. She takes great photos at all the school functions and posts them online. She is well liked by everyone and genuinely seems to like everyone back. She throws great classroom parties—especially for Halloween, where she's known for green "goblin" pudding with a homemade bloody eyeball she makes out of marshmallow and organic strawberry jam. She and her husband, who doesn't look as old as you thought, are the best of friends and often put on family shows on weekends "just because."

The COMPETITIVE DAD. He shows up dressed for whatever high-power job he's heading to after dropping off the kids. He's got them on a short leash, as evidenced by the look of respect/fear in their eyes. He has them playing three to four different competitive sports by the second year of preschool and coaches at least two of them. He walks with a swagger and is often seen readjusting his not-as-big-as-he-thinks crotch through his suit pants. He likes to ask a lot of questions about what *your* kids are doing and at what level in order to create an opening for him to tell you about his. He plans spring break ski trips with the other dads so they can ski, watch sports, get loaded, and talk about which of the moms at the school they'd fuck if they got a freebie. He works hard to stay at the top of his game and keep his family living in a manner to which he's made them accustomed.

The GAY DAD. He falls into any and all of the above categories. Add to that how much he likes to gossip with the moms, flirt with the dads, and croon over the young, gorgeous male nanny. By the way, he heard (and by "heard," I mean he'd like to think) that the manny is also a model and a tennis pro with a nine-inch penis. He also heard that one of the Working Moms is divorcing one of the Competitive Dads over a weekend tryst *she* had with the manny in Vermont. The Gay Dad befriends a circle of moms with whom he can plan playdates and lunches. He competes for friendships with the A-list moms and becomes a shoulder to cry on for the ones teetering on the brink of divorce. The gay dad prides himself on being everything the moms could possibly want out of a man—minus the sex. At the same time, he accepts an invitation for a golf weekend with the divorcing dad. While he doesn't know the first thing about golf, he springs for expensive clubs, shoes, and outfits as a way of jockeying for the approval of these same straight "cool" guys. (These were the guys who shoved his face in the snow as a boy and who now own a shoe conglomerate that could lead to a thirty percent discount on Italian loafers.) The Gay Dad is a devoted parent, shows up to all the kid functions, makes lunches the kids love, and tries to get all their friends to think he's "the coolest dad."

Where do Don and I fit in? I don't know. We're all of them and none of them, smack in the middle of the whole messy parent parade. But looking for ways to evaluate my worth as a parent is a fool's game. I mean, everyone's approach is flawed but valid. And we're all desperate to be the best versions of ourselves we can be.

• • •

A couple of years ago we accepted an invitation for a family brunch date from a couple whose kids were in a summer art class with ours. We enjoyed our giant table for eight and had fun sharing the parental duties, the passing of plates, the cutting up of waffles, sharing crayons, mopping spilled maple syrup—and bringing Jonah back to us after he went table to table to show everyone his yo-yo. It felt like we were all in it together—old school. "It takes a village" and we were a village. Then, something happened. Our new friends, I'll call them Liz and Mike, turned and gave each other some kind of signal to go ahead and ask us what had clearly been on their minds from the moment they invited us for the family brunch.

"Um . . . whose sperm did you—?" Liz was clearly embarrassed but beyond curious. We explained how our kids were part of an adoption plan rather than a surrogacy. They were surprised and impressed that we felt okay about raising kids who had no genetic ties to us. They wanted to know all about our birth mom. They wanted to know everything. I was a little taken aback by the line of questioning but ultimately happy to educate them on anything and everything, as I believe it only helps open the minds and hearts of others. Yeah, well . . . not always.

After we had given them a complete history of how we had become parents, they complimented us on our honesty and our commitment. They were proud to know us, they said. They thought it was "good for their family" to have friends "like us." They wanted their kids to see that the world is made up of all kinds of people and that children can have parents who come in all different shapes, sizes, and genders, as long as the parents love them. We were their "gay dad friends" and they loved us.

I wondered how many other "gay dad friends" they had interviewed prior to choosing us. Granted, the competitive spirit in me was relieved that we had, in fact, been chosen. But then I got annoyed. Were we only friends with them because they wanted a token gay couple in their lives as a teaching moment for their kids? And if that were the case, maybe there was nothing wrong with that. But something didn't feel right. We'd been inadvertently sucked into a strange Playdate Affirmative Action Program. Being chosen or rejected in any work or personal relationship solely on the basis of sexual orientation, race, religion—anything—is the very definition of discrimination, isn't it?

Look. I'm happy to be a role model. I'm happy to be an example to others of the different colors of love and family and marriage. But like everyone else, I'd prefer to be welcomed into another person's inner circle of friends on the basis of my personality or my values, my sense of humor or, I don't know, the whiteness of my teeth?

So what if Liz and Mike wanted to expand their social circle and open their minds to a different type of parent—a modern, less conventional family? I got over my self-righteous outrage and opened my mind and heart a little as well. The conversation ended and we cleaned up our kids and paid the check.

"Oh listen . . ." Mike stopped me on the way to the cars. "I meant to ask you this earlier," he said casually. "You guys don't ever, you know, kiss—in front of the kids—do you? Not, like, by accident or when you didn't realize they're there . . . but, like, if they're having a playdate or anything—you guys don't strike me as the types who are into PDAs? Cool. Just checking." His tone was not one of curiosity. He was asking it like a favor. Like please never do this. I didn't actually say anything in response, but he seemed pretty pleased to have gotten that off his chest. He patted me on the back and headed toward his Dodge Caravan.

And in that moment, the "village" was suddenly down two gay villagers.

chapter twenty-three

Roxanne

After my parent crush on Marguerite Bergman, I shifted attention to Roxanne, whose daughter Lola was one of Eliza's closest New York preschool friends. Our approaches to parenthood seemed to intersect, and I admired the way she balanced the dedication she showed to her kids with the passion she showed in her career as a graphic designer. In my mind Roxanne was doing it all right! We hadn't gotten a chance to really hang out much, though, ever since she'd moved to Northern California after the kids were out of preschool. Fortunately Don and I had to go to San Francisco for an event, so we brought the kids and I finagled a playdate for Eliza and Lola—and for me and Roxanne.

Roxanne, or Roxy, was, like me, a rare hybrid of the Working, Doting, and Perfect/Crafty mom. When we got to the house, she had set up an arts station for each of the kids, complete with stand-up easels, glue guns, and little holsters to hold brushes, markers, and tiny water bottles. If Martha Stewart were six, this would be what she'd design for herself.

"Wow, Eliza! Isn't this great?" I overpraised. It really was quite a spectacle. I was impressed, delighted, shamed, jealous, and enraged by it all at the same time. The kids stayed in the crafts room hand-making their personalized Hello Kitty Japanese bento lunch boxes while Roxy invited me out onto her patio for a glass of wine. It was already five-thirty and I figured a little alcohol would take the sting off my crafts table envy. Roxy's patio overlooked the most perfect, deliberately messy, and overgrown garden of wildflowers I'd ever seen. It rivaled anything Monet was inspired to paint in Giverny. And then Roxy mentioned how she had painted a version of her garden and hung it in her dining room. I had noticed it on the way in.

"That huge painting—the one in the—? Was, wait—*you* did that?" I asked, genuinely incredulous because the painting was wonderful. But Roxy had a lot on her mind she wanted to unload, before I had a chance to compliment her art. She told me how much she loved "the gays" because we're such good listeners.

"Thank you," I said. "You know, on behalf of all us gays." I was being a little facetious, but I couldn't help it. I felt a bit like a toy poodle, sipping delicious Napa Valley sparkling blush in the midst of this stunning garden.

"You know, Rob and I are having sex again," she boasted, absentmindedly playing with a strand of her blond hair. I hadn't realized they'd ever stopped having sex but I read between the lines.

"Oh, wow. Great!" I tried to sound supportive without sounding surprised.

"It's like we just met," she continued, acting embarrassed even though I knew she wasn't. She whispered, "He took me on the kitchen table this morning. Seriously. I found Rice Krispies stuck to my ass when I got in the shower."

She couldn't stop laughing. I was uncomfortable, but I tried my best to laugh along with her. Ha ha ha! I've always liked Roxy, even if she is completely inappropriate. Or maybe because of it.

"It's easier now that the twins are away at boarding school. When the three kids were home it was tough. Someone was always walking in on us—'Finn put gum in my hair,' or 'Lola broke a plate,' or 'Mommy, I have a splinter.' But now, it's like nine-fifteen in the morning and I'm spread-eagle on the kitchen table having multiple orgasms. It's heaven!"

Really? Heaven? I think: *Not for the next people who have to eat at that table.* Actually, *I* just ate at that table.

"Sounds like heaven to me!" I offer. What else could I say? Don and I weren't having sex on the kitchen table. Not that I wouldn't be willing—but really? I'm not twenty. A hard wood table against a herniated disk isn't exactly as cozy as you might think. And Don would never go for it. No, for the kitchen table sex to happen, I'd first have to time travel back before Don was born and have his mother impregnated on a kitchen table herself so that at least the trait would be hereditary. But Don would no sooner have sex that close to cream cheese and strawberry preserves than have sex with a woman.

Roxy looks out over her garden. She reaches out to a baby rosebush beside us and pulls a bloom close to her nose and inhales deeply. I think about how Roxy really lives in the moment, something I need to work *so* much harder to do and often doubt is even possible. But that's how *not* in the moment I was, thinking how *her* smelling a rose made *me* feel like it was something I needed to do more. She was still talking. Had I missed something? This gay poodle was not being a very good listener.

"The only problem is," Roxy continued, "now that the boys are away at school, Lola misses the male attention they used to give her. She needs it. And it's good for her." She looked at me. I nodded. She was still looking at me. Was I supposed to do something?

"If you wouldn't mind, would you say something nice to Lola? Tell her you like her dress?" she asked me, point-blank. I was caught completely off guard. Roxy's eyes were twinkling. I noticed how beautiful she was and wondered how important it was that I notice. Perhaps this was why she wanted her daughter to feel the same way. But the request was so, I don't know . . . curious?

"What? Oh. Yes. It is a nice dress. I'd be happy to," I replied, a little thrown.

"I'm her mother. It doesn't mean the same coming from me. She wants to hear it from a guy."

"Absolutely!" I answered, without thinking twice. Then I thought twice. *What?* Lola is six! Does Lola really need "male attention" at this age? Eliza and Jonah have two dads. Does this mean they need more female attention? My kids have a wonderful female nanny who's been in their lives since they were born. They also have a godmother, Aunt Cuckoo, and three or four other aunts who have been consistent parts of their lives as well. It seemed like Roxy was worried about something and projecting it onto her daughter. Imagine that! And then the obvious dawned on me: that even the seemingly most perfect of parents, who paints and has sex in the kitchen and plants Monet-worthy gardens, is just as crazy as I, and every other parent is. Different crazy. But crazy nonetheless.

The girls came bounding out of the crafts room. Lola hopped into her mother's arms and Eliza into mine. Such happy little girls. May it last forever. Eliza then did what she always does and wrapped my arms around herself super tight. I don't know who loves it more.

"You girls are in a smiley mood. Did you have fun?" I asked. They nodded. Eliza showed me her bento box still wet from the glued-on feathers and glitter.

"It's beautiful," I said, "just like the girls who made them!" I managed to slip in that small drop of "male attention" as promised, but that's about all I felt comfortable with. Plus, it was time for us to go. I kissed Roxy goodbye and thanked her for the wine and the playdate, and the girls hugged.

When we got home, I felt like a new man. Something about being with Roxy made me realize I've been deluding myself into thinking everyone knows something I don't. Maybe I don't need a role model! I *am* a role model. I've got this parenting thing down pat. Don noticed I was particularly chipper.

"What's wrong with you?" he asks, suspiciously.

"Absolutely nothing!" I say, pointedly. Drunk with cockiness about the kind of parent I am, I think maybe I should work on the whole sex-on-the-kitchen-table thing. Right? Why not? No reason why I too, maybe soon, could have Rice Krispies stuck to *my* ass!

chapter twenty-four

Tangled

Eliza and Jonah were quietly watching the final moments of Disney's *Tangled* on my iPad, each with their own set of headphones. Don was visiting his folks in Pittsburgh, so I was flying solo at home in L.A. About an hour earlier, one of the kids had dropped a glass pitcher filled with these horrifically annoying, multicolored, jelly-like pearls the kids *love* called Orbeez. I had a meltdown and put the kids in Disney's hands while I tried to clean the glass and scoop up what seemed like two million beads from every corner of the kitchen floor. When the movie, and my meltdown, were over, I asked the kids how they liked *Tangled*. "What was your favorite part?"

Jonah loved Pascal, the hilarious chameleon sidekick to Rapunzel. Eliza took a bit longer to answer.

"The whole thing," she finally replied. It's her stock answer—her way of telling me to fuck off and stop interviewing her. But then she added, "I liked the part when Rapunzel found the king and queen after she was lost her whole life with the mean lady who wasn't really her mom." And then, after a beat, she added, "I wish I had a mom and a dad." She was still looking down at the iPad.

Straight to the heart, that one. Never thinks maybe pull back a little. Nope. Just straight in and deep. But I knew exactly what she meant. She wants the picture of what she sees in the movies: to be a princess enveloped by her parents, the king and the queen . . . to *feel* like Rapunzel. Or just like most every other girl.

I know she's not sad about the cards she was dealt. But she wouldn't mind having a king and a queen. I suddenly feel sad. For her. For her not being able to have everything she wants, or at least this one specific thing.

Kids need devoted parents who love them and make a home for them. I know that. In my head. But in my heart, I fear that our situation is just a tiny bit not *as* good as if the kids had a "conventional" family. Even though I, like millions of other kids, came from a conventional family and sometimes wished I had it differently. Nonetheless, my heart breaks for my children, who will undoubtedly wish they had a mother from time to time. They'll crave that specific feeling of being embraced by a mommy. But what is that "mommyness" exactly? Can a man bring mommyness to a child's life? I feel that I do. But is it still mommyness if it comes from a man?

A few days after the mommy incident I'm at the playground with a friend, Scott, who is also a gay dad. I ask him if his daughters have ever told him they wanted a mommy.

"Are you kidding? All the time. They're always saying how unfair it is that they can't have a mommy." Scott laughs it off.

"Doesn't that bum you out?" I ask him.

"What are you going to do? Maya also wants a unicorn. I can't pull one of those out of my ass either." Now we both start laughing. Suddenly, a mom from Maya's school inches over to us.

"Hi, Scott." He gives her a hug and he introduces us. "Sorry, I overheard your conversation," she continues, "but I have to tell you, Chloe was just asking me about you and Andrew—and why Maya doesn't have a mother." We both look at her, a little stunned.

"You know what I told Chloe? I told her that some kids don't have any parents at all. So, isn't it better that little Maya has two loving daddies than no parents at all?" She looks at us, so proud of her message. "I think it's great," she adds.

"Thanks!" I think one of us said. I smile at the effort, hiding my inner scowl. She kisses us both goodbye. "So nice to meet you." And then she flies off. But her comment lies there, like a silent but deadly fart. You're not sure you actually heard it but the smell lingers in the air, wet and greasy.

Scott's the first one to speak. "She's not wrong, really. Is she? In a backwards logic kind of way." He's so nice—trying to give her the benefit of the doubt.

"She doesn't know any better," I say. "But she should. Come on, really? Is having two dads only just the next worst thing to having *no* parents at all?"

"I guess if you put it that way," Scott says. "It's not a 'better than nothing' situation, is it?"

Hello! "No kidding! It's better to have only a couple of fingers blown off your hand than lose your whole hand. Isn't it?" I'm on a tear. "She thinks having two dads is like having only a couple of fingers blown off!"

"That's crazy," Scott says.

"Hey. She's your friend." We laugh. "But the silver lining? At least you still have eight perfectly good fingers! And for her you only need your middle one." It's ridiculous. We both know it. And for a split second, I feel sorry for Chloe. 'Cause her mom is kind of lame.

Maybe the thing that makes a kid *want* a mommy is the fact that they see other people who have them and it looks so nice. It's really no different from seeing someone with, say, a new iPad, and coming home to it and being able to play with it and use it and get a bunch of fabulous apps. It's *great* to have an iPad. But must *everyone* have one? Is a life incomplete without an iPad if you have another device that does the same things but only looks different, maybe smells a little different, has a penis, and prefers to sleep with men? Do we need to feel sorry for kids without iPads?

Every kid wants the parents they see on TV . . . or across the street . . . or in the next car over driving their best friend, who always seems to have it better. I'm already jealous of the parents my kids haven't even met yet whom they will wish they could have. I'm jealous of the storybook parents and Disney parents and friends' parents whom they imagine coming home to. And have you *seen* the end of *Tangled*? Those parents rock.

How do I make up for having robbed my kids of the experience of having a mother? I can't. But at the same time, if they'd had a mom, they would've been robbed of the experience of having two dads who love them more than life itself. It is what it is. We do our best and hope that when they grow up, they know they were unconditionally loved. And liked. And respected. And as a result, grow into compassionate, loving, responsible adults who feel lucky with the pair of queens they were dealt.

chapter twenty-five

Angry Bird

I was stepping out of my office the other day when I felt something drop and swoop toward me. I ducked, realizing it was a bird barely missing my head! Afterward, it sat on a branch staring at me, cawing loudly. It wasn't a huge bird, more midsized—bigger than a sparrow and smaller than a crow. About the size of a blue jay. In fact, it looked exactly like a blue jay—only not blue. I laughed to myself at my own jumpiness. It was just a bird, after all.

A few moments later I was returning to my office and the bird squawked loudly, swooped down again, and came right in for the kill. I screamed like a pigtailed schoolgirl, almost squirting myself shitless as I raced into my office. Never shying away from my penchant for the dramatic, I crouched breathlessly by the window to see if I could get a look at my attacker.

"What the hell?" I asked my colleagues. "That bird just tried to kill me!" I was relieved to hear that a few others had experienced the same low-flying bird wrath on their way into the office. So at least it wasn't personal. Then I remembered seeing a dead baby bird in its nest on the ground only two days before. Had this same mean bird attacked an innocent birdlet?

And then it hit me. Not the bird, but the realization: this was probably the mama bird that had lost its baby on the walkway! Clearly working through Dr. Kübler-Ross's five stages of grief, she was currently acting out her Anger Stage at those she held responsible for the death of her young. She might also have been protecting any surviving baby birds still in the nest.

I Googled pictures of birds indigenous to Los Angeles and was fairly certain our attacker was either a mockingbird or a long-tailed bush tit. I could hardly blame our poor tit for her anxiety and rage after what had happened to her child. Nature, cruel as she may be, also provides the parents of each species an ardent protective instinct. My own mother was an "angry bird" of sorts: fiercely protective of her family, vigilant against injustice, and keenly intuitive about whom to trust or not. She's always had a deep-rooted anxiety provoked by worst-case scenarios and an overdeveloped imagination with which to play out said scenarios. I too, sadly, have perfected this mechanism for indulging my negative fantasies.

I was at the farmers' market about a month ago with the kids. I gave them each one ticket with which to do whatever they pleased. Eliza was torn between the petting zoo and the face painting. She really wanted to pet a bunny, but there were a lot of birds in there too—roosters, chickens, ducks, and a pissed-off swan in a tiny inflatable pool of murky water. Fortunately, my kids are scared of birds. Who knows why? They've always thought birds were mean, and that was way before the recent arrival of our psycho mama tit.

The kids stared at the farm animals from outside the

pen. I could tell that even they had stopped thinking it was cute. What the hell is a baby cow supposed to do with a box of bunnies, a rooster, a potbellied pig, and a giant tortoise? How punishing for the animals to be so cramped in such a small Astroturfed pen with so many creatures with whom they have nothing in common! And all of them peeing and pooping on one another as hordes of toddlers tug at their ears.

Finally, Eliza picked face painting and settled in to have her cheeks transformed into an underwater seascape. Jonah chose to use his ticket on the giant tiger slide. For a split second, I turned to tell Eliza to wait for me to return. When I turned back around, Jonah was gone. I raced over to the tiger slide and he wasn't there. I looked around, scanning *every* single stall and ride, and I didn't see him. In real time less than a minute had passed. But to my pounding chest it felt like a lifetime.

My eyes darted as fast as my heart was racing. The blood drained from my face. My mind sped through the story as I would tell it to a sympathetic Ann Curry on a very special *Dateline: Gone in an Instant* about the tragedy I was convinced had just occurred. I'll spare you the details of the candlelight vigil my mind had conjured, and the spontaneous obesity, the messy divorce, and the one-eyed doll they found in the middle of the road (even though Jonah never had a doll, they always find a creepy doll in the middle of the road when a child goes missing). All these images are flooding back to me right now as though the incident had actually happened. But thankfully, it did not.

"Daddy! Daddy! Here I am!" Jonah tugged at my shorts.

I looked down and saw his beautiful face, adorable, spiky blond hair, and that hideously stained *Toy Story* sweatshirt he insisted on wearing. He was real. He was back! I scooped him up in my arms, a little choked up. Even though it had been only thirty seconds since I had lost sight of him.

I plastered a smile on my panicked face. "Always tell me where you are when we're at the market, okay, Jo?" Everything was fine. Everything was going to be fine.

"Okay, Daddy!" he said happily. He squeezed me tightly, sensing my rattled nerves. "I'm okay," he said sweetly. "Can I go on the slide?"

I took his hand as we made our way to the giant inflated tiger, assuring Eliza we'd be right back and she was not to move a muscle until we were.

Having been raised by my mother—who was raised, in turn, by the ultimate worrier, *her* mother—I have no doubt from which family line this particular "panic blood" originates.

My mother and her mother, whom we all called Babe (*Ba-beh*), were both émigrés. My mom came to the United States from Argentina in the early sixties. Her mother had left Poland in the thirties and gone first to Uruguay, then Buenos Aires. It wasn't exactly a cozy time in European history. And Argentina was—well, whatever words best describe the *opposite* of political and economic stability. Every day was a coup d'état-a-palooza. It's no wonder, then, that both these women went through their lives with what I call a *gasp reflex*, normally reserved for seeing a person fall through a sheet of ice or collide with a tree or trip over a pant leg and land headfirst in a wedding cake. With these women, the gasp reflex was activated when a dollop of cream cheese dripped off a piece of toast or when a plate of food arriving in a restaurant was much larger than they'd imagined. (*Gasp!* "That can't all be for me! What? It's too much! *Tell them too much!*") There was never a dearth of drama in my mother's house when I was growing up. I'd like to think there's a little less in mine, thirty years later.

Connecting to the mother in me goes far deeper than my tendency to picture the abduction of my children or gasping at a puddle of spilled maple syrup. I discovered something all parents must feel deep within themselves: a boundless desire and responsibility to nurture and protect. I imagine it's what people call the "maternal instinct." I'm sure countless other men have shared the feeling, which makes me want to lobby to change the term to "parental instinct." What's so female about this feeling anyway? If a sense of *mommyness* is tied to having breasts filled with milk and kids latched onto them for mealtimes, then yes, I'm out. But there's more to it.

In a home where no conventional mommy exists, Don and I, by definition both dads, are freed from the shackles of traditional gender roles and allowed to explore the gamut of parental emotions and impulses. And as gay fathers we have a different challenge, one less obvious. No, I'm not talking about hiding porn. (Though watch out for particularly adventurous and agile little shelf climbers.) More challenging still is finding the balance between the parts of us that are distinctly *dad* and those qualities that are, in a sense, maternal.

I love to roughhouse and play games, carry the kids on my shoulders, put on magic shows for them, and have them watch me while I shave, as I did with my own dad. Put me at a soccer practice or in front of a stack of blocks, a train set, or a Matchbox racetrack, and I'm in heaven. But the feeling of nursing a scrape or holding the kids when they're sick, having them curled up in my lap during story time, or carrying their sleeping bodies into bed, their heads nuzzling the crook of my neck—how do I describe that? Does it need a label? Is that mommyness? Or isn't it all just "parentness"? And can both of us dads play all these roles in turn?

Sometimes Don takes on a more nurturing role, sometimes I do. Sometimes he's the disciplinarian, sometimes I am. I assume this volley of roles occurs in all families—with gay parents and straight ones. But in a traditional male/female relationship, society neatly organizes activities and responsibilities by gender. So no one expects they should be performing a task in the other gender's To Do list.

I walked into the home of our dear friends Michael and Mary, the beloved godparents of Eliza and Jonah. He had his iPad open on his lap while watching a baseball game on the TV, while Mary was running a bath for the kids and had just put a pizza in the oven. There was a comforting predictability to it. It felt appropriate and natural. Despite the fact that both are breadwinners and each has sometimes had to work while the other watched the kids, each tends to gravitate to their more natural, evolutionary role: mom in the hut with the kids while dad is out hunting. Granted, in this case, he was hunting on eBay for a new computer charger. But it was a charger he needed for his work. There is still that very natural, clean division of roles. When Don and I arrived, our kids joined theirs in the tub. I joined Mary in bath-time prep. Don joined Michael in a debate over an external wireless speaker for the TV. But within a few minutes Don and I traded places. Don and Mary dried and dressed the kids, after which Michael and I brought the kids outside for a predinner soccer game.

The lines are blurred in a same-sex marriage. We have the added challenge, or privilege, to expand who we are with our kids. Whether you call it "maternal" or "paternal" care, the kids are getting both. And sometimes there's a bit of a negotiation that has to happen for us to figure out who needs to do what and when. And sure, sometimes that brings up feelings of competition. But usually we know how to defer to each other's particular parental strengths and inclinations.

Don's got a natural "daddyness" gene. He loves bouncing babies on his knees. He loves the sound of children playing while he reads the paper. He throws them in the car to run errands with them or lets them help him wash his car. He's also great when it's time to put a bicycle rack on the back of the car or fix a broken toy. The man was born to use a toolbox and a glue gun.

If it's not obvious already, I do tend to gravitate to a kind of mommyness that Don doesn't spark to. I like getting the kids dressed, cutting their fingernails, laying out paper and paint, and making puppets out of old socks. But most of all, I love cooking with them. And for them. And yet again, this inevitably and predictably links me to my own mother and hers and generations of Jewish mothers before them.

Last weekend, the kids and I donned our aprons and rolled up our sleeves, as we've done countless times before, to make our "famous" banana pancakes. Jonah held the eggs,

Eliza a cupful of batter mix, and I orchestrated the timing of each ingredient. The kids turned away as I mashed the banana with my fingers, as they find it "too grossy." But once the pancakes hit the griddle, the kids ran to their seats and waited for me to serve. There's something that feels so purely uncomplicated and satisfying about feeding my kids—and about the joy it brings them and me.

After breakfast, I opened the kitchen doors to run outside with the kids. In a pocket between a wooden beam and the eave of the roof, we noticed a tiny bird's nest. The kids were freaking out with excitement. I looked over at Don, who smiled, stood up with a sigh, and headed for the garage to get the ladder.

"The nest may be an old one, okay guys?" I felt the need to manage expectations. "The eggs may be gone. Or maybe it's not finished being built. There may be nothing to see. Let Daddy look first, okay? And if there are any eggs, I'll let you guys climb up and look."

Don brought me the ladder and I propped it against the house and started climbing. I feared the worst—that whatever was in that nest had gone the way of the angry tit's chick. I imagined the bird version of a tragic Lifetime TV movie—*If These Twigs Could Talk*—as I walked up each rung. When I reached the top, I looked inside and there, to my delight, were two tiny just-hatched birds.

I brought the kids up to look and they gasped and smiled, whispering "so cute" over and over again. I smiled, thinking *pot calling the kettle* . . . We stepped down and moved the ladder back to the garage. When we came back, we noticed a bird had flown to the nest to tend to its young. The bird was pecking food into the open beaks of the chicks. The three of us just stood there, staring at it—at *Nature*. I was amazed that within just a few days, I had been confronted with the best and worst of it: its arbitrary ruthlessness and cruelty on the one hand, and the beautiful efficiency of it on the other.

Finally, Eliza proclaimed, "That's the mama." She spoke with such certainty, it surprised me.

"How do you know, sweetie? Could be the daddy," I proposed.

"No." Jonah sided with his sister. "The mama feeds the babies."

Eliza nodded. And there it was. I smiled. She wasn't wrong. I looked up at the bird but thought about the sadness of the one outside my office. It's a lot, what life puts us through—us mama birds. It's a lot. But worth it.

chapter twenty-six

Birth Mom Barbie

We had taken a wrong turn at the park one day and wandered smack into a "Pet Adoption Day." It was cleverly decorated with balloons so we joined the other parents cursing under their breath and stopped to look. The kids were jumping up and down to see a lab puppy named Buster, but right away a volunteer was making a hard sell for the "tripod" dog, a terrier mix with only three legs.

"Bugsy got hit by a car and then left on the side of the road like trash. These dogs aren't wanted and then they're abused and discarded until we can get them adopted. That's why Bugsy needs to be adopted. Please adopt her. Adoption is her only chance!"

She said "adopt" or "adoption" no fewer than twenty times. I counted. Don and I looked at each other, praying she'd stop talking. We also were praying this wasn't the one time our kids were actually paying attention to this grown-up continuously linking "adoption" to "trash." That certainly wasn't what our kids' adoption was about. But neither of us is too sure our kids have a full understanding of the word "adoption" in the first place. We both have managed to avoid the word for, oh, six years now.

"These dogs and cats are so lucky! They're in the park today so that they can meet the true parents, er, I mean, *owners* that they were always destined to have!" I say, and make myself a little sick with my over-the-top smileyness.

Don wants to make sure they get the message: "Do you know what 'destined' means, kids? It's when something is meant to be. You see?" The kids are trying to get the puppies to lick their hands. As usual, we were sweating and they couldn't care less. There were puppies!

The story of how Eliza and Jonah came to be our kids is a story we've told them again and again since they were born. But it didn't involve the word "adoption." When Eliza was six months old, we started telling her "the story of Eliza Rose." Every night we'd take her through the little fairy tale and she'd look at us with deep focus and curiosity. We knew she didn't really understand but she loved it nonetheless. It was always the same:

"Once upon a time there were two guys named Papi and Daddy and they were very, very, very happy together. There was only one thing they wanted but didn't have: a baby girl they could call their own. Then one day a girl named Monica called us and said, 'I have just the baby for you and she's growing inside my tummy. And you will be her parents!' So Papi and Daddy went to the hospital and held Monica's hand as Eliza Rose came out of her tummy and into our arms, and we were so happy. But we weren't the only ones who were happy. No. Our dog, Basia, was happy. And your abuela and grandma and grandpa were happy. And your aunts Amy and Lolo and Ruthy and Ellen were happy . . . And Aunt Mary and Uncle Michael were happy . . ." And we'd run down the names of all the important people in her life. (This was our resident atheist Don's attempt to reframe the usual nighttime litany of loved ones that begins "And God bless . . .") When Jonah was born, we told him the story too, with all the necessary amendments. This became our way of sharing with them the wonderfully special way in which we became a family. But we always knew that the story would have to change shape and evolve as the kids did.

We've read and been told how adoption is a complicated issue for kids and you can't predict how they will react as they get older. So we just agreed we'd answer any questions they had honestly. We acted on the belief that if the kids didn't ask, they weren't wondering. Of course that might not have been true. But it was so much easier than trying to guess where they were on the topic and then figuring out how to explain it. It wasn't tricky to explain how they grew out of the love we *and* our birth mom all had for them before they were even born. It will be significantly more complicated when it's time to explain why our two kids are full siblings and have four siblings or half siblings who don't live with us. I can barely wrap my brain around it. I can't imagine how a kid processes that kind of information. It's much easier to say nothing. Or wait for them to ask. Or lie. Or pretend they came out of me.

Standing at the park with all these puppies barking for the chance to live somewhere warm and cozy, it occurred to me that the cute little story we told our kids was no longer enough. I don't remember ever making a decision with Don *not* to mention the word "adoption." We just don't remember ever choosing to mention it. Around the time Eliza was two and Jonah a newborn, a touchy-feely therapist friend bought us this creepy doll named Midge, one of Barbie's BFs, who came dressed in a maternity shirt and a nine-month pregnant belly that attached to her body with magnets. It came with a tiny doll of a baby that fit snugly inside. Riding my newfound determination to explain things to the kids, I decided to get two male dolls to round out the "family." One was Ken, always a classic, and the other was some dude I call Biff. Biff had blond hair, wore two earrings, and couldn't look gayer if he came out of the box with a poodle, a rainbow Speedo, and a real estate license. I sat the kids in front of the dolls and explained how Papi and Daddy were lucky that Eliza and Jonah grew inside Midge's tummy even though they were going to be *our* children. "It's called being adopted. And it's a wonder–"

Eliza cut me off. "Not Midge. Monica!" she said, correcting me.

"Right!" I laughed. "Of course. Midge is just a doll."

"And we grew in her womb. Babies grow in a *womb.* Not in your tummy." Eliza was proud to have so many answers. I was flustered and feeling a little feverish. Maybe playing Birth Mom Barbie wasn't such a great idea after all. I started having second thoughts about introducing the word "adoption" so aggressively. I wisely decided I was in over my head and put the dolls away for the day.

Finally it came up organically when the children were watching the animated film *Rio* (about two dozen times) in which there's a young Brazilian boy, Fernando, who has no family. Amazing how many of my parenting lessons seem to come from cartoons. At the end of the film (spoiler alert) the Brazilian scientist Tulio falls in love with the midwestern macaw-owner Linda, and they adopt Fernando and live in Rio happily ever after. And my kids *love* that part. Out of the blue, sometimes they'll just tell me that Fernando didn't have a family but then Tulio and Linda adopted him and now they're a family.

"That's right! Isn't that so lucky for Fernando? And super lucky for Linda and Tulio!" I may be a tad overenthusiastic. "Who else was so lucky to be adopted?" And both kids smile and shout out their names. It's cute. And I know it'll get tired and old really soon, so I enjoy it while I can.

I started mentioning the *A* word everywhere I could. Like in *And Tango Makes Three*, that fabulous children's book that tells the real story of two male penguins at New York's Central Park Zoo who became mates and nurtured an abandoned egg until they hatched a baby penguin they raised as their daughter, Tango. Of course the idea of adoption will take on more complexity as the kids grow up and start understanding about sex and birth control and wine coolers and rock concerts and reclining car seats. It will be messy for them and possibly even painful. Don and I wonder how it's going to resolve itself. What happens when they're twelve or fifteen or twenty? Will they struggle with a feeling of loss or abandonment as they empathize more with Monica and who she was when she was nineteen or twenty-one, when they were born? Having been through the experience twice now, we know it's never a woman's first choice to get pregnant and then make an adoption plan. It's a solution. Which implies a problem. That's just a fact. As is the reality of that moment at the hospital when the baby goes from the arms of the birth mother into the arms of the adoptive parents: *the happiest moment in one couple's lives is quite possibly the saddest in that mother's.* Even if she knows it was the only and most loving choice she could make. That's why you don't really bring balloons and Mariachi bands into the hospital room with an open adoption. Because the harsh truth is that our blessing was due to our birth mom's misfortune. Makes you wonder, really, about fate or the universe or the existence of God. If there is a God, why would He have allowed her to be in this predicament? Was God only watching over us—to have brought us such happiness? Or, perhaps, it's how one explains what brought us all together in the first place. I'm not sure what I believe. Though I feel certain we wound up with the family we were meant to have.

Monica has always said she felt proud of her adoption decision. She found solace in the knowledge that she was helping create a family for a couple that couldn't naturally. Not only that, Monica would only ever place her child with two guys in a same-sex relationship. She is a real supporter of gay rights and loves feeling like she is helping our cause. But there might have been another layer to it, as well. Many of the birth mothers in open adoption, our lawyer told us, prefer gay men as potential parents as it sort of ensures they will forever be seen as the only "mother." Maybe. Who knows, in Monica's case? Her motives and reasons were her own; we may never know or understand them.

• • •

Jonah recently celebrated his fourth birthday. As we do each year, we got a call from Monica. Jonah grabbed the phone from my hand to say hello to her. He doesn't remember her but knows exactly what role she played in his life. At least as well as a four-year-old knows anything.

"Hi, Monica!" he shouted into the phone. He answered *yes* to a bunch of questions that came after that. Then he started to describe his birthday cake and a few of his presents. And then, after a long silence, Jonah sang out, in his high little-boy voice, "Thank you for carrying me in your womb!"

He handed me back the phone with a swagger, as if to say, *That's how it's done!* Then he returned to his Lego fire truck. And you know what? He meant it. He turned to one of the friends he invited to his birthday party and announced proudly, "I'm adopted. Just like Fernando in *Rio*!"

I smile at Don, so glad the kids were able to embrace the idea in a sweet, uncomplicated way. But then as I look around at the other parents, I wonder if they think I oversimplified the concept. I laugh, nervously, as I suddenly feel the need to explain.

"That's right, Jonah, but you and Eliza were never without a family. You were always wanted, right from the beginning. Actually, Fernando was wanted too. By his family. Before he lost them." Jonah looks up at me, confused. I'm getting tongue-tied.

"No. No. It's okay," I try and reassure him. "After his parents died, maybe Fernando was left without . . . he didn't have anyplace to go." The kids stare at me, frozen. What had I done? Don went to get the cake. So I was on my own to dig the foot out of my mouth.

"Oh, it's a *nice* story. Because he wasn't living in the streets very long. At all. I mean, sure, he did turn to crime.

And he was thin, but not really starving or sick like a lot of homeless kids—" Jonah actually starts to cry. Eliza isn't far behind him.

"Kids! It's a happy ending because Linda and Tulio adopted Fernando . . ." It's no use. The kids don't like the word pictures I've created. At long last, I let it go and announce, "Time for cake, everyone!"

I thought about Ken, his partner Biff, and Birth Mom Barbie. Maybe I was the one who needed them all along. Because as is often the case, the kids know better than the parents. While the story is complicated, the truth is quite simple: "Thank you, Monica, for carrying them in your womb."

chapter twenty-seven

Why Are We Still Talking About This?

I'm Jewish. And I have the big hair and subsequent flatiron scars to prove it. And of course the embarrassing Bar Mitzvah pictures with me in a brown, three-piece Pierre Cardin suit surrounded by a gaggle of pubescent girls in braces and beige gauchos towering over my squat four-eleven frame. My bar mitzvah was an important milestone in my life. Not because I read from the Torah for the first time or was seen as a "man" in the eyes of my people. It was a huge party with dance games, a cake in the shape of the classic theater masks (hello?), and the first time I was able to get Joe DeCarlo and Eric Stempler to show up to one of my parties. They were the most popular guys at school. That felt really good.

My Jewishness also included celebrating the major holidays when I was growing up: Chanukah, Passover, Rosh Hashanah, and Yom Kippur. We never fasted, but it was still a tough day, as my dad would sequester himself in the den and cry, remembering his parents, both of whom died when he was in his early thirties. We'd go to temple for the Kol Nidre service and I would count the lightbulbs in the synagogue while some lady played the Kol Nidre prayer on a cello. There was never a dry eye in the house. Although *my* tears were from boredom.

Like most Jewish Americans, we were in it for the cultural experience rather than the religious significance. Like Tevye in *Fiddler on the Roof*, it was all about *tradition* and the connection these rituals seemed to have to those who came before us, especially for all those who perished in the Holocaust. It was not about God.

We never talked about God. In fact, when it came up, both my parents made it pretty clear they were atheists. Actually, my dad was more of an agnostic, as he'd often concede that we'd never really know about the existence of God but he believed in "something"—maybe a fourth dimension or what he'd describe as "the unknown." Despite their skepticism about religion and the existence of God, my parents did send me to Hebrew school where I learned a few songs, some unlikely biblical stories, and how to sneak out of a bathroom window.

As an adult, once I moved to Los Angeles I continued to celebrate the holidays in my own way. I'd surround myself with others who'd grown up as I did and occasionally crash a temple service for the High Holidays. It's something I've struggled to maintain, especially once I was in a relationship with a Catholic, albeit a lapsed one. Don, more than anything, is a devout atheist who recoils at the thought of any organized religion. It's gotten so bad lately that Don roots against any reality show competitors, regardless of their dance abilities or swimmers' bodies, who invoke the name of God in the outcome of their game. Oh, how he relishes his Schadenfreude when they are eliminated—laughing as they explain away their misfortune as "His will." Needless to say, the notion of raising my kids as strictly Jewish was off the table. But while Don would happily avoid the whole area of religion altogether, he's been cooperative in helping integrate into our lives the traditions most important to me.

Since the first year we met, we've always celebrated Passover. The first year, I was only twenty-eight and used the seder as an opportunity to come out of the closet to some of the extended family and friends that still didn't know. That particular seder went down in family lore as the "gayder." For over twenty-five years I'd sat at the Passover table, only now I had my boyfriend next to me. I was a nervous wreck, convinced the pink elephant in the room had upstaged the story of our people being freed. I was representing a different "people" that night and my stomach was doing backflips. Finally, I mustered my courage and pulled my aunt aside before dinner to tell her I was gay. I thought the worst was over, but the actual meal was torture. Why was this night different from all other nights? Gee, I don't know, let me think. Maybe it's because all my relatives are imagining me with a penis in my mouth!

It got easier as the years progressed. Don joined me as a regular at the table and now we continue to travel east for the holiday with the kids. And now that my father is no longer with us, my sister, her husband, and I run the seder as a team.

The kids and I also celebrate Chanukah every year, lighting a menorah on most of the eight nights. I say the prayer and the kids love having an extra holiday and extra presents!

Make no mistake, I love Christmas. I love getting a tree, trimming it, putting up stockings and all those gorgeous twinkling lights. When I was a kid, I tried to contain my enthusiasm and sell the Chanukah bush idea to my parents with a minimalist design, only silver and blue balls, white lights, and a simple Star of David on top. But once I married a goy I went hog wild (I know, not kosher) with the multicolored lights, elaborate ornaments, and inflatable Santas in every window! There is nothing quite like the fervor of a Jew celebrating Christmas. We get to throw all our neurotic and obsessive attention to detail into a holiday that was kept from us as kids. And now with small kids, I get right in there with the Santa hat, the plate of cookies for him, the caroling, and the stockings hung by the chimney with care.

At no point has the question of God ever come up with the kids. They haven't asked and we haven't been in any hurry to explain it. Don would undoubtedly call it "mumbo jumbo," which would probably call into question other childhood myths. Neither of us ever wanted to lie to them. But we realized that cheating them out of the stories of Santa and the Easter bunny and the Tooth Fairy would also be cheating ourselves out of their wide-eyed wonder when they'd talk about them. Their imaginations run wild with possibilities of how they enter the house and leave treats for the kids while they sleep. Our children believe with an enviable commitment. It makes me want to believe like that—in something. Things got a little tricky when the pets died. "Where are they?" the kids asked. We told them they were dead. But "dead" isn't an easy concept for children when they're so little. We swallowed hard and said, gently, "We don't know. They stopped living and now they aren't here anymore. That's what 'dead' is." It would have been convenient to talk about God and Heaven and angels, but that wasn't going to happen in our house. At all. And the kids were fine.

So this year when I had the opportunity to bring the kids to a friend's temple for a very sweet, family service for Rosh Hashanah, I thought it might be a nice way to introduce them to a tradition from their daddy's childhood. Understandably Don didn't want to go but was very open to my taking the kids: "Have fun getting into tight pants to expose our kids to black magic!"

Within a few minutes of our arrival, the congregation began singing a familiar Hebrew prayer and I found myself singing along. In fact, I knew most of the songs. And while the Hebrew meant nothing to me in a literal sense, something about knowing the words and melodies made me feel a sense of belonging not just to the rest of the congregation and to my family but to hundreds of years of tradition that came before me. I looked over at my kids. Eliza was listening and mouthing the words she pretended to know. Jonah had his yarmulke over his face. I used to do that. For a second, it even looked like he was counting lightbulbs. I wanted to remember this moment forever. I was overcome with an enormous wave of humility and gratitude. Gratitude to whom or to what? That's a bigger question.

For the moment, let's put aside all the debates over how or what we teach the kids—how much we compromise on TV viewing, how much sugar to give them, and how it all impacts whether they become crack whores or not. Put aside my petty preoccupations over whether to straighten my hair before the parent/teacher conference or whether the skinny jeans I just bought are age-inappropriate. Notwithstanding all that, I do know this: I love Don enough to respect his refusal to believe in a force great enough to create if that same force is cruel enough to destroy. And Don loves me enough to respect my belief in some inexplicable force that gives us the strength and courage to take on the greatest of life's challenges: from the very decision to start a family by making an adoption plan, to the treatment of a congenital heart defect, to the challenge of keeping our kids' fingers out of every orifice of their bodies with love and without shame. Add to that all the daily triumphs and defeats that come with being a human being on a planet with children who all at once make us feel immortal and remind us that we aren't.

The kids and I hop into the car after the service. I can't help looking at them in the rearview mirror. Stay in the moment. Right now it's just about us, driving in this car, enjoying this gorgeous day. We're on our way to meet Don for breakfast. We're going to get pancakes. It doesn't get better than this.

We get to a stoplight and a homeless woman walks up to the car, holding a sign that says PLEASE HELP. NEED FOOD. Eliza notices her first.

"That woman doesn't have a home or a car, right, Daddy?"

"That's right, sweetie. That's called 'homeless,' remember?" We've discussed this many times before. I'm acutely aware of the opportunity to turn this into a "teaching moment."

"We have a house and a car," Jonah adds, straining his neck for a peek at the homeless lady.

"That's right, Jonah. What do you think about that?" I ask. They don't answer. "You think it's fair?"

"Where did she get the cardboard and the marker to make her sign?" Eliza asks. I stifle a laugh. It's a good question.

"She probably borrowed them from someone who was willing to help," I say.

"Or she stole it," Eliza says. There is a lot of sibling toy stealing in our household, and a lot of lectures about its evil.

"Maybe," I say, "but if you had cardboard and a marker and she needed one, wouldn't you lend them to her?"

"Yes," Eliza says. The moment seems to be over. The kids are now looking out the other window.

"Can you think of different ways a person could help another person who wasn't as fortunate as you?" Beat. Beat. The light turns green. We start moving. It's still quiet. "What do you think, kids?" Still nothing. "How would you help that woman, Eliza?"

Innocently, her blue eyes peeking out from under her blond Dutch-boy bangs, she speaks.

"Why are we still talking about her?" she asks.

I burst out laughing.

"What?" she asks, puzzled. "Can you just turn on the music?"

"What's so funny?" she asks again. Jonah starts laughing too.

I laugh and laugh, tears rolling down my cheeks. Eliza is telling me we didn't need to make a "moment" out of a stoplight and to let things just be. In the words of Anaïs Nin, "We don't see things as they are. We see them as *we* are."

Maybe Eliza is more of a Jew than me, and anyone else in my family, for that matter. Not only is she Jewish, she's a little blond fifty-pound rabbi! Like Ecclesiastes, she knows there is a time to talk and a time to listen, a time to teach and a time to learn. A time to stop thinking and a time to play music. "Just turn on the music," she says again. And I do.

ACKNOWLEDGMENTS

I never set out to write a book. Not originally. Until now, I've always been a writer of made-up worlds, with made-up characters who do a bunch of things in between a lot of commercials. But then I had kids and my life expanded. And I was encouraged to write something truthful by Beth Lapides to perform at her show *Say the Word.* After that, I had the good fortune of meeting Dani Klein Modisett, who created a platform for other writer/performers and authors and comedians called *Afterbirth: Stories You Won't Read in a Parenting Magazine.* I will forever be grateful to Dani for the opportunity, the inspiration, the encouragement, the guidance, the collaboration, and the friendship.

A word of gratitude to Matthew Benjamin, my editor at Touchstone Books, without whose steady, levelheaded, and patient manner (I know, that's three adjectives, bad habit) I couldn't have written this book; and to everyone at Touchstone and Simon & Schuster for giving me this opportunity of a lifetime. Thanks to my agent, Kathy White, and my whole team at CAA for the constant support and encouragement for anything and everything I dream of doing; and to my literary agent and Vassar classmate, Simon Green, who always had his eye on the bigger picture and saw a book in all these stories.

And speaking of my Vassar connection, I am forever grateful to my business partner and friend of more than ten years, Lisa Kudrow. I could never have taken on the challenges of a book like this without her support, enthusiasm, thoughtful feedback, and sense of humor. Thanks to my assistant, Kyle McNally, for his limitless support, patience, and intelligence and for never letting me forget he went to Yale.

I want to thank Dan Savage. For paving the way. For inspiring us to have kids. And then teaching us all it's okay to talk about it. All of it. With humor.

To Ivone Del Cid, the fifth member of our family from the very beginning and forever more. Eternal thanks to Dr. Stephen Gordon for, well, saving our daughter's life. And David Radis. And Dr. Stephen Rabin and Vista Del Mar Child and Family Services. And Shandiz Zandi, my safety net.

I'd like to acknowledge Amy, Lorin, Grayson and Gus Flemming, Robert and Ellen—for being the family I feel so lucky to have so close . . . and across the country: the Migler family and Norm and Marilou Roos, who continue to be such wonderful grandparents to our kids.

To our dear friends Mary McCormack and Michael Morris, who raise their kids (our godchildren) with ours (their godchildren) and in doing so redefine the boundaries of friendship and family. I want to thank Susan Gauthier and Linda Wallem, our beloved "tier one," for thinking Don and I might make a nice couple twenty years ago and Jodi Binstock for joining the efforts. Ann Donahue, whom I met that same fateful night, and Anne McGrail—writers and parents with whom I'm so lucky to experience parenthood and Christmas Eve!

Amy Poux, who's inspired me the longest—since I played Lysander to her Helena in the first grade. Terrence and Tom. Our dear friends who continue to set an example of true commitment not just to love and marriage but to the power of the written word. I also want to thank friends and colleagues from whom I've derived so much guidance and reassurance for so many years: Thea Mann, the very definition of family. And Nicole Tocantins, Tim Bagley, Tony Phelan, and Joan Rater; Suzi Dietz, Caroline Aaron, Krista Smith, and John Hafter; Andrea Martin, Victor Garber, Rainer Andreeson, and Deb Monk; Linda Lowy and Jeff Perry; David and Bob Schneiderman; Eric Mathre and Peter Levine; Joe Fay and Matt Shay; Devin Keudell and Audrey Wells. And Lisa Melamed, for all her expertise, gossip, and—the title! Thanks to Ayelet Waldman and Craig Chester, who've done it all before and talked me off ledges and encouraged me to trust in the truth.

To my parental inspirations: Steve and Sylvie Rabineau. Like a brother and sister on the West Coast, you have a way of just making me feel like everything's going to be okay and, along with Julia and Brad Hall, made us realize what's possible, and doing it with such patience, class, and humor.

I want to thank my dad. For coaching all who knew him how to truly savor life. I miss you more than you'll ever know. I want to thank my sister, my best friend, my role model and reality check, and my cheerleader (Varsity *and* JV). And my mother, Myriam. Thanks for being relieved when I came out of the closet. And for the tears of joy when we said we wanted to adopt. And for the years since—as a devoted "abuela" to our kids without letting us forget the spirit of Abuelo.

And I want to thank my husband, Don Roos. For twenty years you've put up with my particular brand of crazy. You laughed at my jokes. You made me feel young-er than you. Since I am. By ten years. And taught me the difference between working hard and working smart: You've made me a better writer; a better partner, friend, and husband; and now a better dad. And Eliza and Jonah: you are my life. I can't wait to see you every single morning when I wake up. Of course without you there'd be no book. You've changed me. Deeply. And you keep teaching me new and deeper meanings for the word "love." Yes. Even more than pad Thai.

ABOUT THE AUTHOR

Dan Bucatinsky wrote, produced, and starred in the indie romantic comedy *All Over the Guy* (Lionsgate). In 2003 he and partner Lisa Kudrow founded Is Or Isn't Entertainment, which produced the cult HBO comedy *The Comeback*, costarring Bucatinsky as publicist Billy Stanton. Their acclaimed docuseries *Who Do You Think You Are?* recently completed its third successful season on NBC. The pair have also garnered critical and audience attention for the groundbreaking web-to-TV series *Web Therapy* on Showtime, in which Bucatinsky also stars. Is Or Isn't Entertainment also joined with film producer Marc Platt to produce the 2010 independent feature *The Other Woman,* starring Natalie Portman and Kudrow, directed by Don Roos. As a writer/producer Bucatinsky co-executive produced the NBC dramedy *Lipstick Jungle.* As an actor, Dan appears on the new Shonda Rhimes series, *Scandal,* and returns as well to the USA series *In Plain Sight.* Television audiences will also remember him from *Grey's Anatomy, Curb Your Enthusiasm,* and *Weeds.* Film roles include *I Love Your Work, Under the Tuscan Sun,* and *The Opposite of Sex.*

One of the 2011 recipients of Power Up's Ten Amazing Gay Men awards, and the Out 100, Dan lives in Los Angeles with his husband, filmmaker Don Roos, and their two kids. He can be followed on Twitter: @danbucatinsky.